Words of praise for YO

"*You Can Let Go Now* will help you let go of who you are so you can become all you can be. Jacob's quest for significance will enlighten you and help you begin your own journey of letting go."

—John C. Maxwell
Founder, The INJOY Group

"It is said that the marble contains the image; the true sculptor simply releases what is already in the marble. Dr. Chironna's life quest is to help each person within his sphere of influence enjoy the delight of 'becoming.' It is not diffi-cult to communicate the principle of individual uniqueness; but Dr. Chironna excels where others stop: He teaches you how to find fulfillment in your cre-ated purpose, by letting go of the façade of comfortable acceptance and grasp-ing firmly the true, principle, authentic existence that alone guarantees wholistic fulfillment: You have to become comfortable in your own skin."

—Bishop Joseph L. Garlington, Sr., PhD

"Mark Chirrona has written a practical masterpiece to cause us to cease strug-gling to be who we already are! Once we have discovered who we are in Christ, we then unlock our infinite potential of what we can do and find peace with ourselves, God, and others! *You Can Let Go Now* is a 'must read' revela-tory book which concisely addresses our most basic need for true identity."

—Bishop Dale Carnegie Bronner, D. Min.
Senior Pastor of Word of Faith Family Worship Cathedral

"Dr. Mark Chironna has the ability to mine out the hidden gems of Scripture stories and bring things to life that we always believed, yet never quite could put into words. The hidden treasures in the story of Jacob's transformation from someone who was always the underdog to someone who became the father of a nation are placed in your hands in this book. *You Can Let Go Now* will revolutionize your faith, unlock the door to your identity and destiny, and take your walk with God to a whole new level."

—Larry Huch
Author of *Free at Last*
Senior Pastor, New Beginnings Christian Center

"Many books claim to give you inside insight into the mind of God. *You Can Let Go Now* will give you inside insight into who you are really supposed to be. Mark Chironna has a prophetic voice that will illuminate the pathway to your own destiny. Read it and reach to your destiny."

—Tommy Tenney
God Chaser Network

"Dr. Chironna is a master at communicating God's truth in such a way that four-thousand-year-old truths come alive, as he merges them with today's culture. His prophetic gift, along with psychological insight, and deep understanding of the Word of God, provides a unique blessing to the Body of Christ. This book will challenge you to let go and let God develop the real you."

—Jeff Hackleman
Family Faith Church
Huntsville, Texas

"Mark Chironna's intuitive style again calls us to look beyond the surface to the 'me that only God knows.' We are so often trapped by outside symbols, titles, and positions. Few are those who really love 'us' simply for being . . . 'us.' Thanks be to God, Mark Chironna has called us back to the remembrance that we are but dust and clay.

I commend this thoughtful work to readers everywhere who recognize that we are all more than what meets the eye and that it is finally okay to be who God intended you to be."

—Dr. Donald Hilliard, Jr.
Cathedral International
Perth Amboy, New Jersey

"Dr. Mark Chironna has written an uplifting book taking us on a spiritual journey of how the transforming, powerful love of God can turn hatred into love and forgiveness through Christ our Lord."

—Rhonda Fleming

"Becoming fully alive and true to your God-given potential and destiny is what Dr. Mark Chironna's latest book is all about. His insights into the transformation of Jacob and his journey from being a heel-grabber to being a prince will bring you to a place where you too will want let go of what is no longer serving your true identity and empower you to be who you were created to be in God."

—Paul F. and Jan Crouch
President , Trinity Broadcasting Network

"When you are around Dr. Mark Chironna, or partake of his ministry, you'll know that he is a man who has a personal relationship with God. His revelation of the Word is incredible. His knowledge of God is evident. He elevates all who hear him. When he speaks of the new creation, you truly experience being more than a conqueror. He demonstrates the love of God when ministering to hurting people.

With joy I commend Dr. Chironna. His books, tapes and CDs bless everyone around the world."

—Pastor Gerald Hilley
Eastgate Church, Dayton and Webster, Texas

"Do you want to know who you are, why you think the way you think and why you do what you do? This book will enlighten your understanding of these questions. Take a look through the pages as Dr. Chironna unveils keys to free you from you."

—Bishop Eddie L. Long
Senior Pastor, New Birth Missionary Baptist Church, Lithonia, Georgia

"Once again, Mark Chironna skillfully leads us where few have dared to trek, into a world of recovery, security, and unlimited possibility. This author is uniquely qualified, in that he has been there before us exploring the way. He writes from a first-generation revelation of what life can be when we recover our memory and become who we already are in Christ."

—Dr. Terry Crist
Pastor, CitiChurch International

"This new book by Dr. Chironna, *You Can Let Go Now*, is a must-have-in-your-library for not just the church and secular communities, but also for the business leaders and those aspiring to become great in their world seeking to find true fulfillment and destined purpose in their lives.

This book will inspire, challenge, encourage and push you out of your comfort zone of believing that someone else on this earth is destined to find your purpose, and fulfill your destiny for you. You are designed by God to find your purpose in Him in spite of your inner fears and insecurities. . . Read this book and search the inner soul for some long-awaited answers that you never knew existed. Let go and live."

—Bishop Henry Fernandez
The Faith Center

"Dr. Mark Chironna is a friend whose life, dedication and commitment to God have made an impeccable mark on my life. Dr. Chironna has once again caught the heart of God in helping those who are held captive by the past to soar into their God-given destiny. The message of *You Can Let Go Now*, is an invitation to let go and let God. These lessons from the life of Jacob are relevant, and more importantly, revolutionary to every believer. As you take hold of these truths and let them get on the inside of you, they will change your life. In this great book, Dr. Chironna will help give you a glimpse of just how great your life can become, because your life is your future."

—Sam Hinn
Senior Pastor, The Gathering Place Worship Center

"It's a great pleasure for me to endorse this book for Mark Chironna. I have been acquainted with him down through the years. He's a man of integrity, and anything that he writes will be a blessing to all the people of God. I trust that you'll be blessed as you take time to read this material."

—R. W. Schambach, Evangelist

"Refreshing. Brilliant. Scholar. Communicator. Liberator. Visionary. Leader. Change-Agent. These descriptors barely scratch the surface of multi-gifted Dr. Mark Chironna. In *You Can Let Go Now* you will discover all of these and more. Go mining for these endless treasures. Dr. Chironna is a unique gift to the Kingdom."

—Dr. Samuel R. Chand
Chancellor, Beulah Heights Bible College, Atlanta, Georgia

"In his desire to see God's power touch the human condition, Dr. Mark Chironna has combined his years of study with powerful biblical truths. The result is a spiritual roadmap on the journey to deliverance. Here is how you can enjoy full freedom through Jesus Christ!"

—Ted Shuttlesworth, Evangelist

"While reading this book, you will discover the encouragement, strength and peace needed to focus on the questions you have been feeling but unable to articulate. As the answers begin to unfold, you will discover *You Can Let Go Now*.

Trust Dr. Mark Chironna, an anointed individual, to help you loosen the grip on things that have had a grip on you for far too long. In your hands are the answers to the questions you've been feeling."

—Bishop David G. Evans
The Abundant Harvest Fellowship Of Churches

"Captivating. Dr. Chironna grabs my heart and leads me to places that satisfy the deepest longings . . . in ways I could never have described to myself. Helping us believe again in the possibilities of life is the unique gift of this man; a renewed focus on the adventure of life is on every page. Read this book with a pen and your journal close by . . . there are truths here that are foundational to a fulfilling and successful life. Grab life and live!"

—Paul Louis Cole
President, Christian Men's Network
Southlake, Texas

"Mark Chironna could write anything, and the Body of Christ should sit up and listen. Here is a revelation from the heart of a man who lives with a passion for the things of God."

—Pastor Wendell Smith
Senior Pastor, The City Church

"When you think of Jacob, you either say 'Oh my' or 'Oh me.' He is a colorful character filled with potential, strength and destiny. However, there is a part of us that always relates to his dark side. He usurps! He struggles! He manipulates! He plays favorites! He fails! But God ... He causes Jacob to triumph, overcome, and become! This book is wonderful. These are days of letting go and becoming who we are for the future. *You Can Let Go Now: It's Okay to Be Who You Are* is the word for the hour. God did it with Jacob, and He can do it with you."

—Dr. Chuck D. Pierce
President, Glory of Zion International Ministries, Inc.
Vice President, Global Harvest Ministries

"We are called human beings. But we constantly try and get fulfillment out of doing, not being, and until we learn to enjoy being, we will never enjoy doing. So, it is not just a curiosity but a necessity to learn who we are. Then you will be victorious at whatever you do. So, you will need to read this book, and then Go and Be!

My wife and I have been in the ministry 23 years, and when Dr. Mark Chironna prophesied over us, it was the same as the first time we heard God speak to us about our ministry. I knew it was coming from God because Dr. Chironna said some things that only my wife and I knew. Like they say in the world, it was as if he was reading our mail. It gave us new encouragement and enlarged our vision, and got us fired up to go on for the Lord. Thank you, Dr. Chironna, for your ministry, and for your friendship

Dr. Mark Chironna is a fire starter. Every time he comes to minister at our church, he leaves a fire behind. Thank God for fire starters!"

—Pastor Wayne and Monica Cochran
Voice For Jesus Church, Miami, Florida

YOU CAN LET GO NOW

IT'S OKAY TO BE WHO YOU ARE

Mark J. Chironna

OLIVER
NELSON

NELSON BOOKS
A Division of Thomas Nelson Publishers
Since 1798
www.thomasnelson.com

Published in Nashville, Tennessee, by Thomas Nelson, Inc.

Library of Congress Cataloging-in-Publication Data

Chironna, Mark J.
    You can let go now : it's okay to be who you are / Mark J. Chironna.
        p. cm.
    Includes bibliographical references.
        ISBN 0-7852-6233-4
    1. Self-realization—Religious aspects—Christianity. 2. Jacob (Biblical patriarch) I. Title.
    BV4598.2.C45 2004
    248.4—dc22

                                                                    2004015515

Printed in the United States of America

04 05 06 07 08 PHX 5 4 3 2 1

CONTENTS

Contents

CHAPTER 1 | WHEN WILL IT BE OKAY FOR YOU TO BE YOU?

It was Emerson who said that most individuals lead "quiet lives of desperation." How often we settle for less in life while our hearts cry out for more. We arrive here by mystery and miracle from a watery womb, and when we break forth out of our safe, specific environments the first thing that emerges from the depths of our spirits is a cry. It is our primal expression of being, a first demonstration of our awareness that something traumatic has taken place and that there is no longer room for us in the individual worlds in which we were formed.

We haven't got a clue about what life is supposed to be, yet we exhibit patterns and behaviors long before we ever say our first words. These patterns and behaviors seem to have a mind of their own, a script they are following, with or without our permission.

We learn that our primary sound, that intense cry, gets all our needs met—milk, a change from wet clothing, and whatever else our little hearts demand. It works really well, at least for a little while. There does come a moment, though, when our

1

parents shut our bedroom doors and ignore our cries. So we cry even louder, and it doesn't work. This is very frustrating.

We soon discover we have hands and fingers, and they are quite effective at grabbing things. As a matter of fact, we take all that energy that we used for crying and invest it in each of our five fingers.

Then one morning we are invited to drink our milk out of a cup. Growing up and making the journey isn't comfortable to begin with, and now it seems to be getting worse. In anger, we each may grab that plastic cup and throw it back. We may even grab hold of those high-chair trays hemming us in and shake them in hopes of freeing ourselves from their clutches. We are grasping and grabbing with everything we've got, because we aren't allowed to do what is most comfortable for us, or be who we have been up to that point. It is no wonder that Peter Pan preferred the Island of Lost Boys to a life of growing up and becoming all that he was supposed to become.

No one else can make our journeys in life for us. We have to find our own way through the maze of life, seizing what is most important and essential by the choices we make. No one else can achieve those levels of mastery for us.

At times we fail miserably. Yet at other times we seem to momentarily grasp a sublime realm of possibility that far exceeds our wildest imaginations and dreams. Those deep yearnings, those urges that demand fulfillment and expression for your uniqueness . . . where are they living in you? They come from a place deeper than your understanding, deeper than your words can describe. They don't even ask permission to invade your waking hours or your sleeping seasons. They just show up, from the time you are little, like an uninvited guest at dinnertime.

Those deep yearnings, those urges that demand fulfillment and expression for your uniqueness . . . where are they living in you?

Somewhere on the journey from childhood to adolescence, you either seek a way to make those dreams and yearnings fit into the real world that seems so contradictory to the one you envision, or you bury your flights of fancy and chalk them up to childhood foolishness. Instead of capturing what those dreams really were pointing to, you may grab on to shoddy substitutes that keep your hands full and your heart empty.

You reach a rite of passage when you buy your first car. Now you really have something that proves you have "made it." Then you get a flat tire or have your first fender bender. Later you finally buy your dream home and get a zip code that says you are some kind of somebody, and then your roof leaks, and your maintenance costs increase every year.

While your hands have finally encircled the things you thought would make you feel great about who you are, your heart is still aching for something deeper and more enduring. You live experiencing the gap between your expectations of your reality, and the reality of your expectations. No matter how hard you try, the gap is too far for you to bridge with your grasp, your grip, your fingers—because what you want is out of reach.

You want to stake out your unique dreams, while at the same time you may fall back on your fears of failure and success, which amount to the fear of being all alone. You may want what you don't have, have what you don't want, and become torn between which option provides the greatest rewards. One is the reward of comfort and safety; the other is the reward of risk and opportunity.

You also want to know that you are significant, and that your life is essential to some greater purpose. Some people become holograms, or more literally, "hollow-grams." They look real, touchable, approachable, and three-dimensional, yet they are empty and hollow and in need of substance—the substance of true identity.

Your real primal cry is the cry to know *who you are*. You and I believe that security, accomplishments, and things will give us identity, yet the more we struggle for identity, the more it eludes us. It isn't until we are free to let go of the grasping and the grabbing that we find out who we truly are.

So where do we go to find the answer to our dilemma? When is it safe to stop snatching and clinging? Where do we solve the problem of being who we truly are? Do we know who we truly are? When is it okay to let go and be who *you* are?

Within the pages of an ancient manuscript, there lies the story of a grappler, a grabber, a clinger, whose life becomes a model of the pathway to well-being, wholeness, true-to-God self-worth, and authentic identity that indeed is destiny. The grasper's name is Jacob, and his name actually means "heel grabber."

Even as early as Jacob's development within his mother's womb, it was never okay for him to let go. He gripped, clenched, and kept on clinging—until the day he discovered it really was okay to let go of the hollow, needs-driven life he was living. When he found out it was okay to let go, his nobility and princely character emerged, and a prince who prevailed with God and men became a model of uniqueness, authenticity, and greatness for generations to come.

There is a genuine, spontaneous, and fully alive *you* deep inside that has been eagerly awaiting an opportunity to show up and live life to the fullest. The God of Jacob is still available to form you into that noble, authentic, true-to-God self, that person who has been crying out to be free since the day you arrived on the planet.

As we look at Jacob's story, you, too, will discover that there will come a defining moment when *you* can let go, because it will finally be safe for you to be who you were meant to be, and who you truly are!

CHAPTER 2 | WHEN YOU CAN'T LET GO OF YOUR DOMINANT NEED

Afterward his brother came out,
and his hand took hold of Esau's heel;
so his name was called Jacob.—Genesis 25:26

Life purpose is about knowing who you are, and that requires knowing to some degree where you came from. Without those clear points to track your life—where you came from, where you are, and where you are headed—you can wrestle with everything until someone finally gives you the answers you are looking for.

Author and anthropologist Gregory Bateson once said, "It takes two to know one." In other words, you can't know yourself *by* yourself. On the stormy seas of life, when you get thrown into deep waters, you can't throw yourself a life preserver, because you aren't built to live this life by your lonesome. You know yourself in relation to others.

Even God said, "It isn't good for man to be alone" (see Genesis 2:18). So you need others. The challenge is whether or not you enjoy being around all the others in your world. If you could only choose with whom you arrive on the planet, and who raises you, and who grows up with you, it would be great, wouldn't it?

The naked truth, though, is that you really didn't have a choice in where you came from, who may have arrived here with you, and to whom you arrived. In the ancient story of the patriarch Jacob, we have twin boys born to a mom and dad late in life who were just so thrilled to have children that they weren't really prepared for the gift they were given.

It's a strange thing to look carefully at the day that Isaac and Rebekah's twins arrived. The pregnancy was far from easy for Mom, and even though she had prayed for years to have a child, when she finally became pregnant, she got double for her trouble. She felt as if there was a war going on below her navel—and there was. Jacob and Esau weren't simply twins; they were two nations at war even before their armies existed. Talk about a tough pregnancy! When the day came for Rebekah to finally deliver, I am sure she was relieved. But that was only the beginning of this family drama—or comedy (or both, depending on how you want to look at it).

Who was this twin brother who emerged from the womb, clutching the heel of his older brother? What was the reason for his intense urge to grab his brother and not let go? Where did he get his *chutzpah*?

There are no accidents. Twin brothers, born of a formerly barren womb, fighting for supremacy even before their birth—

it all had a hidden meaning for Rebekah, for Isaac, and most importantly, for the twins.

God has a purpose for everything, and everything has its purpose for God. Everything in life has a purpose, even if it isn't evident at first. Every blade of grass, every snowflake, and most importantly, every human being, including *you*, is born for a great purpose. And the quest for meaning, the search for significance, and the hunger to know who you are, where you have come from, and where you are going, are amazing parts of the human experience.

THE DOOR TO YOUR DREAMS

Time after time in life, you will find yourself seeking to give expression to that deep inner urge for meaning and significance and fulfillment. This desire is much like a key, and we might call it your *golden key*. It is a particular shape and cut, unique to who you are, that searches for the lock and the door—the door to your dreams—and it fits perfectly.

The challenge is that along life's journey you find yourself trying to make the key fit all sorts of doors, only to discover that it doesn't work . . . yet! Rack up enough unopened doors and you can grow disillusioned with the prospect of ever finding the "right door." The key ends up being something that gives you more pain than pleasure.

Like Rebekah, what you hoped was going to be the fulfillment of your biggest dream became a nightmare. Instead of

9

peace, you are at war within yourself. And like the younger of the twins, you emerge from the dark womb of your internal conflict with your hand clutching the thing that is getting in your way. Yet the more you grab it, the more power it seems to have to prevent you from getting to where you want to be.

Rack up enough unopened doors and you can grow disillusioned with the prospect of ever finding the "right door." The key ends up being something that gives you more pain than pleasure.

CONFLICTING NATURE

A baby is the miraculous result of combining the mother's and father's DNA. Think about that for a moment—each child is a unique blend of the parents' genes. Fraternal twins, like Jacob and Esau, are simply two siblings conceived in the same womb at the same time. How can two babies conceived from the same parents, born at the same time, and raised together, have such opposite personalities?

I once heard someone say that there is both a warrior and a peacemaker inside every one of us. Each demands the right of expression, but they are on opposite ends of the spectrum when it comes to how they express themselves. Yet somehow we need to figure out how to get them to reconcile.

Have you ever been through a season in your life when you discover that parts of you are in conflict? A part of you wants to make sure everyone in your life is happy, while another part cries out, "When is it okay for *me* to be happy?" Half of you wants to be sure that everyone likes you and approves of you, and so you do everything possible to make sure that no one can find fault with you. Meanwhile, the other half is tired of living up to everyone else's expectations.

On the one hand, keeping everyone else happy enables you to live in the illusion that the world is peaceful, but it also causes you to bury your real feelings. The end result is that you are stressed out, burned out, and maybe even physically ill because you have piled a bunch of stuff on top of your deepest yearnings in an effort to avoid the pain of being alone.

What you fail to face you cannot erase, and it will show up later on at the most inconvenient time and season in a way that makes itself so obvious that you won't be able to stop running from yourself. Admiral Perry, upon entering the waters surrounding Japan during World War II, said, "We have met the enemy, and he is us."

The opposite natures of Esau and Jacob came from Isaac. Isaac passed on more than his genetic history: he passed on his own pain, his own unfinished business, and his own inner conflict.

Now it came to pass . . . that God tested Abraham [Isaac's father] . . . He said, "Take now your son, your only son Isaac, whom you love, and go to the land of Moriah, and offer him there as a burnt offering . . . So Abraham rose early in the morning and saddled his donkey, and took two of his young men with him, and Isaac his son, and he split the wood for the burnt offering, and arose and went to the place of which God had told him.

Then on the third day Abraham lifted his eyes and saw the place afar off. And Abraham said to the young men, "Stay here with the donkey; the lad and I will go yonder and worship, and we will come back to you."

So Abraham took the wood of the burnt offering and laid it on Isaac his son; and he took the fire in his hand, and a knife, and the two of them went together.

But Isaac spoke to Abraham his father and said, "My father . . . Look, the fire and the wood, but where is the lamb for a burnt offering?"

And Abraham said, "My son, God will provide for Himself the lamb for a burnt offering." So the two of them went together.

Then they came to the place of which God had told him. And Abraham built an altar there and placed the wood in order; and he bound Isaac his son and laid him on the altar, upon the wood.

And Abraham stretched out his hand and took the knife to slay his son. But the Angel of the Lord called to him from heaven and said, "Abraham, Abraham! . . . Do not lay your hand on the lad, . . . for now I know that you fear God, since you have not withheld your son, your only son, from Me.

Then Abraham lifted his eyes and . . . there behind him was a ram caught in a thicket by its horns. So Abraham went and took the ram, and offered it up for a burnt offering instead of his son.
(Genesis 22:1–13)

While Isaac appears to be a docile and peace-loving figure in this account, even to the point of submitting to a trek up a mountain and a silent yielding to be a lamb led to slaughter, he evidently had a wild side that he never expressed. Esau is the evidence of that wild side.

Everything in the universe has its opposite: night and day, the heights of the heavens and the depths of the oceans, winged creatures that fly and finned creatures that swim. Everything in your internal universe also has its opposite. The presence of hope implies there is the possibility of despair. With the potential of love, there is also the possibility of indifference, even hatred.

> The presence of hope implies there is the possibility of despair. With the potential of love, there is also the possibility of indifference, even hatred.

We would not be fascinated with the story of Dr. Jekyll and Mr. Hyde if it did not speak to something inside of us. That reality haunts all of us from time to time. Paul said of his own internal struggles: "For that which I am doing, I do not understand; for I am not practicing what I would like to do, but I am doing the very thing I hate" (Romans 7:15 NASB).

None of the patriarchs are presented as flawless, even when they are at their best. Thankfully for you and me, that provides us a realistic lens through which to view our many selves. And, yes, there are many selves that we carry around inside of us. There is the *you* that you allow others to see; the *you* that you hide from everyone else, and the *you* that you have never even known is there.

There is the social you that is all wrapped up in who you relate to, and you may even have a different social self for different situations. Remember how, as a teenager, there were ways you carried yourself in front of your parents and ways you carried yourself around just your friends? Believe it or not, you may still be doing the same thing as an adult.

There is the biological you. This you includes all the various seen and unseen parts of your physical nature, and if one of those parts is damaged or has to be removed, it affects how you view yourself.

There is also the you that is identified by all the material things you own or wear or have accumulated—your profession, your salary, your house, and even your car.

Then there is the you that *you* think you are. It may be a you that is always at the top of your game, or it may be a you that is always sad. It isn't the real you; it is the you that you created.

However, there is another "you" that often goes undiscovered, and that is the essential you, the spontaneous and free you, the spiritual you that longs to be known. That you, however, hasn't ever been given the opportunity to show up at social gatherings. It is the you that nobody knows, not even yourself. It is an incredible you, an ineffable you, and as the song says, an embraceable you. Yet it is also the you that is so deep and so far from words, memories, accumulations, and the images you project to others that it evades your grasp. You want to grab hold of it and get a grip on your life, yet it is elusive. You know that this part of you is there, but it is so far beyond the other company of "yous" that it is buried beneath them. Like Peter Pan's mischievous shadow, the harder you seek to grab for that deeper, essential you, the more it stays just beyond your reach.

That you is looking for a connection to a world where it can finally grow up and come out of the darkness. It is also the one that you are most afraid of. It was Nelson Mandela who said, "It is not our failures that frighten us, but our potential for greatness. We fear authentic greatness far more than we fear our failures and shortcomings. We fear the kingly and queenly parts of ourselves because the other parts of us are so demanding that even if that royal part of us were to emerge, the other parts of us would surely seek to destroy it."

Isaac, Jacob, and Esau all carried things inside them that needed to be free. Yet it was Jacob, the most driven of the three, who would emerge as the model for becoming truly authentic. It was Jacob who would generate the nation that possessed the land of promises. In his healing there would also be healing for his father and his brother.

We are not always aware that we are seeking to be healed and made whole. It is a noble thing to embark on the healing journey, yet not all of us do so, even if we deeply long for, even crave, that wholeness. Some of us fear that we will be pursuing a false hope, because people don't change; others are convinced we don't have what it takes; and some of us feel we have tried and failed so many times that we can't handle another disappointment.

What began in Paradise with our original parents, Adam and Eve, eventually ended in a dark place where there is sorrow and sighing, regret and disappointment. Adam and Eve gave in to the temptation to doubt the incredible goodness of God as a caring Parent. When you question God's goodness as a caring Parent, you develop suspicions about life itself, as well as about God. You have to then assume total responsibility for everything to be good in your life. You have to "look out for number one" because no one else is looking out for you. That choice leads to all sorts of added disappointments and difficulties.

As you know, the story of the fall of man tells us that Adam chose to eat from the Tree of Knowledge of Good and Evil in order to become "like God" (see Genesis 3:1–6). Any effort to do something to become like someone else has its roots in that original decision. Adam and Eve were already created in the image of God. What drives us to seek to add to what God's goodness already has done?

Temptations and drives come in all shapes and sizes. The need to prove ourselves is not new to the human race. Whatever it is about our inner experience that leads us to attempt to validate our existence is at the core of what separated Adam from the true essence of his being in God.

The journey to wholeness and well-being is the journey to knowing ourselves as fully integrated human beings. It is about coming to a place where there are no longer any enemies within. I speak here of conflicting parts within yourself, and not interference from without by the forces of darkness. However, it is helpful to realize that oftentimes conflict in the soul opens the door to harassment from the forces of darkness, which seek to take advantage of our pain, our brokenness, and our unresolved issues. Coming to a place of wholeness, of genuine internal integrity, leads to freedom from those powers of darkness that seek to oppose and hinder your pursuit of true self-worth and lifelong satisfaction.

INTERNAL INTEGRITY

A fully satisfying and abundant life is a birthright; however, it requires knowing who you are. And that requires getting real about all the conflict that goes on inside of you.

Integrity comes from the Latin *integra*, which means "whole." Internal integrity is all about internal wholeness and well-being. It's about having all the parts of you coming together to a place of peace and alignment. No, it isn't about inappropriate behaviors and things that are destructive. It is about realizing that if you keep running from all those parts of yourself, you will keep reaching for the one part of you that refuses to be grasped.

Have you ever had a dream in which faceless people surrounded you? Is it possible you were dreaming about unknown parts of yourself—wonderful, rich parts? Have you ever had a dream in which you were being chased by someone and couldn't run fast enough to get away, only to find that when you stopped running and turned around to face your pursuer, your fears subsided? Are you running from a part of yourself that you need to be reconciled with? What is it about all this that is crucial to abundant living? Without internal integrity there is no external integration.

Internal integrity is achieved when everything inside you fits together and flows together from your thinking to your feeling to your doing and your saying, and ultimately leads to external integration. External integration is when everything on the outside fits together, flows together, and comes together to serve you and support you in pursuit of your life purpose. When you are in a place of internal integrity, you will discover that the external lines of life fall to you in pleasant places. All the pieces of the puzzle start to come together on the outside when everything on the inside of you is fully connected and integrated. Internal integrity leads to external integration!

YOUR DOMINANT NEED

Knowing God is crucial to knowing yourself. More specifically, knowing God as the caring Parent that He is, is essential to knowing *your* true and deeper self. However, the process can be a bit of a challenge, since God chooses more often than not to hide, so that we might seek Him out and make discoveries along the way not only about Him, but also about ourselves. Often God takes great delight in staying hidden and requires you to make connections between where you have come from, where you are, who you are, who else is connected to you, and what you sense at a deeper level. Psalm 14:2 says, "The Lord looks down from heaven upon the children of men, to see if there are any who understand, who seek God." God is pulling you to become authentic, fully human, and fully alive.

It isn't all that easy to let go of your dominant need. To attempt to fix yourself from your own limited awareness only invites temporary relief from the all-too-common human ailments of anxiety and despair. At some point you may reach out for help. You may unknowingly cling to whatever or whoever is closest to give you what you need most: a sense of knowing who you are, where you came from, where you are going, and the reason for your existence.

Deep down in your soul is the God-given hunger for authentic identity. Jacob grabbed for a thousand and one things until he finally got hold of total unconditional acceptance. Once he had his hands on it, he couldn't seem to let go and was afraid that if he did, he would lose what he had been looking for all his life.

Somewhere deep in the divine blueprint of your heart lies the awareness that your identity is indeed your destiny. I would like to suggest that really knowing who you are at the core of your being *is* your dominant need. Tell me, how can you let go of that? Someone once said, "If you are born a king and don't know you are a king, then you are not a king. If you are born a king and *know* you are a king, then indeed you *are* a king!"

At the core of your being, you are spirit. Your essence is not material, not physical, and not able to be measured. You are far more than the air you breathe and the blood that circulates in your body. At the center of your being, you are more, so much more, that to explore the depths of that "more" requires connecting with the One who is Spirit, in whose image you were made. That is your dominant need!

THE IMAGE MYTH

Have you noticed how image conscious society has become? It has gotten in the way of your authenticity. If idolatry exists in our day, it is present in our tendency to imitate someone else. We change our appearance and adapt our behavior and speech patterns so that when people finally connect with us, they get someone else! Idolatry is simply hand-me-down living. It is at the core of the pursuit of a "self-image." We have become so image conscious that we attempt to remake ourselves so that others will find us acceptable.

Self-image is not something to work on; it is something to let go of! It is a false fabrication of your own making—a projection of your inauthentic "hollow-gram." It has no substance and no reality whatsoever. When you equate self-image with genuine self-worth, you are comparing apples to oranges. They are worlds apart. One is inauthentic (self-image), while the other is a powerful feeling of respect for who you truly are. Yet how can you feel respect for who you are if you don't even *know* who you are?

> Self-image is not something to work on; it is
> something to let go of!

Someone else has to affirm you for who you are at the core of your being, and until that affirmation comes, you will grasp at anything that you think can tell you who you are. Your dominant need causes you to live life grabbing at the heels of anyone you believe is one step ahead of you. If anyone is one step ahead of you, that individual's feet must know the way, so the best you can do is grab that person's heel and attempt to either get ahead of that individual or be dragged with him or her into the future. However, whose future are you moving into when you grab at someone else's heel?

THE POWER OF A NAME

When the second son of Isaac emerged from the womb of Rebekah, they labeled him "heel grabber." What kind of satisfaction and fulfillment can there be for someone who is "named," more accurately "labeled," after his behavior? Aren't you *more* than your behavior?

Isaac and Rebekah did the best they could at the time. Yet they had a limited viewpoint from which they named both boys. Those names, those labels, became their "identities," their "images." The older was simply named "hairy," which is what

Esau means. Whereas Jacob was named after his behavior, Esau was named based on an aspect of his outer appearance. How limiting is life when you are labeled based on your outer form? Isn't there more to you than meets the eye? Culture often glamorizes external images. In our culture the "perfect" image is someone with a slim waist and the torso of a Greek god or goddess. That image is shallow and empty. It is a "hollow-gram," for sure.

Are some people "shallow" simply because they have been told again and again that there isn't much depth to them? If you are going to fulfill a self-fulfilling prophecy, make sure it is beneficial and meaningful and in line with your true-to-God identity, otherwise you are inviting a greater level of pain and suffering into your life. Living up to an "image" that is less than the true-to-God image will always bring pain.

Jacob's name was a label that became an identity; that indeed evoked a limited destiny. It became a stigma the young lad had to live with for a long time.

Living up to an "image" that is less than the true-to-God image will always bring pain.

"Sticks and stones will break my bones, but words will never hurt me." Nothing could be further from the truth. You can far more easily recover from the wound of a stick or a stone than you can from what a word, a label, a name, invokes in your life.

YOUR TRUE IDENTITY

Driven by the unmet dominant need to be affirmed for who you truly are, you spend a great deal of time in your developmental years attempting to prove who you are *not!* Someone says, "You don't have what it takes to do this," and automatically something in you grabs on to that, and you won't let go until you prove that, yes, you can (whether or not you really can!). You want to be seen for who you are, heard for who you are, and most importantly, accepted for who you are. But when you discover that in order to be accepted there are certain rules you are expected to follow, you learn how to suppress who you really are.

You begin to build an entire inventory of what it takes to be accepted, recognized, understood, welcomed, and celebrated. You build your "self-image wardrobe." You learn how to play the game, suppress your feelings, deny the hurt that causes your tears, and get on with moving through life.

When you are driven by that dominant unmet need, it is difficult to be conscious that you are limiting your life by choosing behavior that is not affirming. You aren't in the driver's seat—your unmet need is! You actually end up continuing to choose behaviors that diminish you rather than expanding and enlarging you.

You see everyone through the distorted lens of your unmet need. You even project all that stuff onto God. You learn to live with feelings of regret and disappointment and become convinced that even God doesn't take notice of your struggles.

Remember, you were made in the image of God in a way that is unique to the vital design of the life you were born to live. Your key won't work when you attempt to fit it into the image of someone else's lock. You cannot copy someone else's life. You have to become true to your own identity, because your true identity, or more appropriately, your true-to-God identity, is your destiny.

Here is the bottom line: you cannot let go of your dominant need to be affirmed for who you are until you know who you are. And you cannot know who you are until you have a deep encounter, perhaps even a wrestling match, with the One who made you. The vital design of your life can only be affirmed in the presence of the vital Designer!

Please remember this: as every key is made for a specific lock, *you* have been made with a design that is so unique it cannot be duplicated. If you fail to be who you truly are, then you will deprive the world and yourself of an incredible gift that was intended to bless many.

As hard as Jacob may have attempted to get ahead of his brother by grabbing at his heel, the best he could do was frustrate himself and set himself up for further disappointment. His real struggle wasn't in the hand he used to grab his brother's heel; it was in the part of his heart that was seeking to reach for his destiny, yet didn't quite know where to find it. What did he do? He grabbed for the first thing that stood in his way.

When you do that long enough, and refuse to get in touch with why you are doing it, you can convince yourself that everyone else is going to get what is rightfully yours, and you will miss your opportunity to find the doorway to your dreams. Let go of the lie that you can never lay hold of your heart's dreams. Reject the lie that everyone is out to deny you of your true-to-God existence. Let go of the belief that the struggle is with someone else; it is with yourself. Cheer up; you can and will let go, and your deepest longings will be satisfied!

CHAPTER 3 | WHEN YOU CAN'T LET GO OF YOUR NEED TO COMPETE

When the boys grew up, Esau became a skillful hunter, a man of the field; but Jacob was a peaceful man, living in tents. Now Isaac loved Esau, because he had a taste for game; but Rebekah loved Jacob. —Genesis 25:27–28 NASB

I can remember from very early in my childhood hearing the question, *what do you want to be when you grow up?* And from my earliest recollection, I wanted to be a doctor, because that is what my father wanted me to be. Dad's presence was so vital to my life that I wanted his approval more than anything else in the world. He told me from the time I was young that I was going to be a medical doctor and I simply accepted that that was what *I* wanted to be. I didn't understand way back then that Dad had broken dreams in his own life. Becoming a doctor wasn't my dream; it was what Dad had wanted to be.

By the time I was "grown up," which I used to think was when I became of legal age, I painfully had to admit to myself that all those years I spent answering that question about who I wanted to be when I grew up had now caught up with me. The answer I had always given no longer rang true. I didn't want to be a doctor. I was tired of preparing to live someone else's life. Yet I so deeply loved my father that I had great difficulty sorting through how to be who *I* was without breaking his heart.

There is something about a dad's approval that is inseparable from being a son, or even a daughter for that matter. Dads have the ability to make you feel that you are the greatest thing since sliced bread. On the other hand, sometimes they can make you think you are an accident waiting to happen. When a dad's unfinished business remains alive and well and is never owned, he can easily pass that unfinished business on to his kids, even if that isn't his intention. I am not saying a mother can't do the same thing, but there is something about the deep father hunger in us that moves us to want our dads' approval no matter what, even at the expense of our own identities. Isaac's own deep need for his father's approval—his "unfinished business"—was passed on to his sons and caused conflict.

Isaac himself had spent most of his life being everything he thought his father, Abraham, wanted him to be: peaceful and obedient. However, Isaac also had an older brother, Ishmael, who was a great hunter and a "wild man" (see Genesis 16:12; 21:20–21). Even though Ishmael wasn't around when Isaac was growing up because of a family feud (Genesis 21:9–14), their dad probably talked about him a whole lot. And why wouldn't he? Ishmael seemed to represent that wild and untamed side of Abraham that loved the hunt and had a taste for game.

> When a dad's unfinished business remains alive and well and is never owned, he can easily pass that unfinished business on to his kids, even if that isn't his intention.

There had to be nights in the tent and by the campfire when Abraham reminisced about his other son, the hunter, the wild man that he deeply loved and had a difficult time letting go of (there is that letting-go thing again). Oh, those stories Isaac must have heard about his brother who didn't have to live according to the same rules. Those comments like, "I wonder what my son Ishmael is doing now." There had to be something those conversations sparked in Isaac about living a life opposite to his own submissive one.

What effect might that have had on Isaac? Does anybody know for sure? Well, the evidence seems to be that there was a wild side that never got satisfied in him, because when he was finally out on his own and had his own family, he reproduced that wild side in his son Esau. Esau was that unspoken cry of Isaac that never had the chance to find expression.

Both Esau and Jacob grew up and became what was most natural to them. Yet only one of these sons appealed to Isaac. Isaac was not impressed by what Jacob was doing with his life. It is even evident that Isaac was indifferent to his second-born son. Remember, the opposite of love is not always hate, but indifference. Isaac loved Esau because Isaac had a taste for game. In other words, there was a "wild" side to Isaac that he was hungry to satisfy. This side of him found fulfillment in Esau's performance as a hunter. Esau's life met an unmet need in his father, but nothing Jacob could do was enough to satisfy his father's taste for the wild things in life.

Well then, who was Jacob? We know from the story that he was a "peaceful man." The word in the original means "having integrity" or "being whole." There is an interesting thought: this one who is labeled a "heel grabber" is actually described as being whole and having integrity. So many scholars take great pains in describing how much of a cheat and a conniver Jacob was, yet few bother to look at this written record of his deeper nature. He was a man of peace with some degree of integrity—yet he didn't have his father's love, acceptance, or approval.

What do you do when you are denied the thing you want most? Jacob could tell you: you strive for it. If he could just figure it out—he hoped—then his father would notice him and approve of him. How he longed for the blessing of his dad. Sadly, however, Isaac never really approved of Jacob. Perhaps it was all too painful for Isaac to accept Jacob for who he was. The reason? Maybe Jacob was so much like the Isaac that had to be peaceful and submissive for his own father's sake that Jacob was a constant, painful reminder of himself.

Rebekah, on the other hand, deeply loved Jacob, because

she knew what God saw in the lad. She also knew before he was born that Jacob was destined to be the heir apparent to the blessing and the birthright.

After a long bout with depression and despair from not being able to have children, Rebekah found that when she finally conceived, the pain was so bad that she would have preferred never to have been pregnant at all. During that troublesome and restless season, Rebekah cried out to God in desperation, "why?" She was given a revelation that there were two nations in her womb, and they were already battling for supremacy. Yet it would be the younger son who would be the heir of the birthright and the blessing that began with Abraham. (See Genesis 25:22–23.)

Rebekah had received a word from God that the younger son would be cared for, seen, recognized, and honored for who God had made him to be. She could already foresee from the beginning that each son would war for the affections of the parent who preferred the other son. Each would war for the right to be seen, heard, and accepted, and both would war for the right to be blessed.

It isn't conceivable that Rebekah would have kept silent about her revelation from God. She must have shared it with Isaac. Yet tragically, Isaac apparently dismissed it as irrelevant, and perhaps chalked it up to the hormonal changes that Rebekah endured during her pregnancy. We don't know for sure. Yet we do know that their subsequent actions and behaviors in relationship to the boys indicate that Rebekah chose to

31

honor what God said, while Isaac chose to honor what met his need for the unexplored wild side in his own life.

Rebekah chose to honor what God said, while Isaac chose to honor what met his need.

There was no way, from Isaac's point of view, that a son such as Jacob could be the powerful heir apparent of Abraham's blessing, so he ignored Rebekah's claim of a divine revelation. It was clear to Isaac that Esau was the "most likely to succeed"—he had what it took. Jacob could only come alongside and offer the vegetables to the real meal. The order was clear: Esau was the heir apparent. He was the firstborn, and he was the strong one.

How did the boys "grow up" then? Perhaps they never did. Oh, they may have grown up physically, and even mentally, yet they never grew up as a real family with one intent and purpose. This was not the perfect family—far from it. This was a dysfunctional, real-life family with real-life human struggles and temptations. There was a vying for affection, and there was competition for attention by the boys. The brothers grew up hating each other; no indifference here.

Jacob was rehearsed again and again the prophetic promise God had given his mom, and she continued to let him know that all that mattered was what God had in store, even if his father never quite celebrated his performance. Jacob was indeed driven, yet he was driven by something beyond what was visible to the naked eye. He had an eye for the inheritance. Weak as he was in the natural, he had the makings of a mighty warrior in the spirit, who could be driven by the value of the greater promise. Jacob was motivated by a world beyond his natural eyes—where a prize awaited the one who could prevail in spite of all the odds, and bring out of the invisible what he innately knew was there. In all of Jacob's scrambling for his father's attention, in all his scratching and, perhaps, scrapping to compete with his brother, there was a deeper motive: his hand was seeking to reach into the realm of the unseen and bring into solid reality the blessing of the firstborn in spite of all contrary evidence.

THE SNARE OF COMPARISON

Jacob didn't yet fully have that assurance that what God had for him was indeed for *him*. He knew that his mom had *told* him that God had reserved that blessing for him, even though he wasn't born in the right order to get the birthright. But he didn't know how that would be worked out, and didn't understand why things always seemed so tough for him—from the time he was a young child, when it came to his relationship with his brother and his dad.

It isn't safe to let go of competition, you know, unless you are freed from the power of comparison. As long as you are driven by the need for approval, you will find yourself either comparing yourself to someone who, in your perception, is getting the approval you want, or you will find that others demand that you "measure up." Either way, the systems that you are a part of can either support that dysfunction or heal it, depending on how fully awake and aware the people are that make up that system.

If the system is built on comparison, competition is the only way you will ever get attention. That is how the misguided world works. "Why can't you be more like your brother?" it says. So you learn how to play the competition game simply to survive. You end up believing that the way to soothe the pain of comparison is to simply compete all the harder, hoping that one day you will win the attention and the endorsement that you crave. You grasp at the "heel" of whoever it is that outperforms you, comparing yourself to him or her.

Sadly, even if you do win once in a while, it only lasts until your need to be noticed and validated pops up again. And since the culture that teaches you how to compare hasn't changed and actually expects you to be conformed to it, you start that vicious competition cycle all over again. Your need for recognition, approval, and affirmation won't go away by competition. It will only intensify.

When the culture that squeezes you into its mold is built on comparison, you either become a slave to its grip or you let go. But you can't let go unless you know there is something you can replace it with that will meet that deep need. *When will it be safe to let go of the need to compete? When will it be okay to stop comparing yourself to others?*

CHAPTER 4 | WHEN YOU CAN'T LET GO OF YOUR NEED TO HAVE IT ALL NOW!

And when Jacob had cooked stew, Esau came in from the field and he was famished; and Esau said to Jacob, "Please let me have a swallow of that red stuff there, for I am famished." Therefore his name was called Edom. But Jacob said, "First sell me your birthright." And Esau said, "Behold, I am about to die; so of what use then is the birthright to me?" And Jacob said, "First swear to me"; so he swore to him, and sold his birthright to Jacob. Then Jacob gave Esau bread and lentil stew; and he ate and drank, and rose and went on his way. Thus Esau despised his birthright.
—Genesis 25:29–34 NASB

All this business about a birthright seems so far removed from our high-tech society, doesn't it? What was the big deal about all of this birthright stuff? It is simple, really. And don't kid yourself—even though most families don't necessarily talk about birthright issues in our culture, just watch what happens when the patriarch or matriarch of a wealthy family passes away and all the siblings fight over the estate or contest the will. Nope, things really haven't changed all that much in the human condition.

The birthright was all about the special privileges and advantages of being the firstborn in the lineage of Abraham. Among other things, whoever was the recipient of the birthright became the priest of the family when the father passed away. If you happened to be in a rather large family, that gave you weighty influence. Influence can be wonderful if you want to inspire others to reach their ultimate good and best. Influence driven by a need to have power over others, however, can be quite destructive.

I will never forget my high-school Western Civilization teacher drumming British historian Lord Acton's words into our brains: "Absolute power corrupts absolutely." You have to be careful about the fine line between having influence and having a need for power. When you have genuine influence, you can make the world a better place to live for lots of people. The power you have is then born out of your integrity and your commitment to the good of the whole. It isn't about satisfying your own unmet need to be important. Power is a by-product of genuine influence and is effective when used wisely. Power isn't meant to be an end in itself.

The discovery of the power unleashed when an atom was split at the dawn of the twentieth century was never intended to be used to wipe out two entire cities in a moment of time.

This scientific discovery was intended to launch us into an age of creativity and peace for all mankind. Instead it became a device for keeping the drive for conquest and power in check, depending on who has the latest technology that can do the most destruction. Power can be quite intoxicating, to say the least.

Wounds in relationship to a father's approval are often behind both the efforts of high achievers and overachievers, and even, in some cases, brutal dictators. Hitler's personal history and his own private wound in relation to his father led to his bloodthirsty reign of terror. Some of the greatest leaders in history had a need to find authenticity in the eyes of their fathers. Winston Churchill is an interesting study in the wounds of a heart that never felt it received the real approval of a father. Churchill lived with depression and a deep need to prove himself worthy of his father's blessing. At the end of his life, he still wasn't sure his life had counted for much, though history considers him one of the greatest leaders of the twentieth century. Yet that mattered little to his own heart. All he ever wanted was his father's recognition and approval.

When you get into the life of Jacob, that is really what he wanted more than anything else. He was willing to do just about anything to get it. It wasn't power for the sake of power; it was power for the sake of getting his father to see him for who he was. And, by hook or by crook, that birthright was going to get him what he wanted: the "A-OK" from his dad.

SECURING THE FUTURE

Since the future is where you are going to spend the rest of your life, it is important to make appropriate decisions now, that don't violate your own internal integrity, based on where you deeply long to be. You can eventually run from everybody else that you take advantage of, but you can never run away from yourself.

There is a lot at stake when it comes to fulfilling your destiny and designing your life based on values and ultimate objectives. When you are so interested in making sure you secure your future "no matter what," sometimes you'll do things that you wish you'd never done. It's okay; we all do those things on the journey toward genuine wholeness and well-being. We all make mistakes, and we all need to know we are still loved and accepted.

You can eventually run from everybody else that you take advantage of, but you can never run away from yourself.

Seizing your moment when it comes requires not only being aware of your moment when it arrives, but also being aware of what matters most in the larger scheme of things. Somewhere inside each of us there lies this strange skeleton in the closet. We don't like opening that closet, yet we know what is in there—and it has an effect on everything we think, say, do, and feel. That skeleton is the remains of a part of each of us that refuses to believe that God is a good God and that He is up to something really wonderful in our lives. We have suspicions about the goodness and faithfulness of God, so we choose to rely more on our own shrewdness than we do on childlike trust in a good God.

This is so engrained in us that we do our darnedest to secure our future, with or without God's help. We want to have it all, but we also feel guilty about it. Why? Because somewhere inside we know that if we really intend to have it all, it can't be had by manipulation or deception, regardless of the folks who appear to get ahead in life doing those sorts of things. And yet, when we feel that nobody is looking (even God), we go ahead and risk doing a few things for ourselves to secure our future, because, after all, if we don't look out for number one, who will? Certainly God has too many other things on His agenda to be able to sort out every little detail of our lives. And if God wants us to have it all, and promises us an abundant life, why wait? Let's get the getting while the getting is good.

When you hold on so tight to the desire to have it all—and have it all right now—you can lose sight of the big picture. Here is the shocker: you really *can* have it all; you just can't have it all at the same time. Jacob eventually got it all, everything that was promised him and then some. Oh, it came with lots of heartache and pain, but he got it all. Then he had to learn many lessons along the way so that he could handle it all. Perhaps the biggest lesson he learned was that he couldn't handle it all, all at once. It takes time to learn how to handle your inheritance, your birthright, your brightest and best expression of your highest hopes and dreams.

BEING NUMBER ONE

What was the actual "moment" that Jacob grabbed hold of? The twins were constantly at war for the affection of their father. The older never had to work for it but wanted to keep it; the younger worked hard and never got it. Had Jacob only stopped to look at his brother's life, he might not have wanted his position so desperately. Here is the mighty hunter Esau, the pride of Isaac, the son on whom the sun never set for Dad. Yet for all his prowess, his skill, his wild and untamed nature, there was a part of him that wore out easily and contradicted the façade of the "machismo" he projected. Esau was the kind of guy that everyone thought had his act together.

Here is the rub: it is tough being number one. You have to work really hard to stay there. If these two boys were fighting for the number-one position even in utero, what does that tell you about Esau? We know Jacob wanted to be first, and we are told that God promised he would be first. What about Esau? He actually *was* first and *was* in line for the birthright, yet his twin brother still wouldn't let go of his heel. Through the years, he was constantly grabbing at his brother and clutching his heel, so to speak. He did it in his behavior, he did it in his conversation, and he also did it in his silence. Esau, as strong as he was, was being worn down by the presence of the guy in second position who wanted to be in first.

In the 1960s there was another type of competition going for the position of "number one." Back then, Hertz dominated the rental-car market. You couldn't even think "rental car" without thinking Hertz. Hertz continually told the public, "Let Hertz put *you* in the driver's seat *today!*" They also had a small yet powerful trailer statement that always followed. It wasn't deceptive; it was true, and it was powerfully seductive. Guess what that statement was? "We're number one."

How could any other company ever hope to gain a position in a free-market economy in the rental-car business when the competition was already number one in the eyes of the public? The owners of Avis, a young and hopeful car company, wondered how Avis could ever hope to be number one, since the position was seemingly already taken. But some ingenious marketer sat down with them and basically said, "Forget trying to get the number-one position. Take a different approach." Some of you may be old enough to remember what that approach was. It actually became the turning point in their business, nationally and internationally. It was a slogan that has stuck and remained, and it was based on an attitude. It connected with the buying public and gave Hertz a run for their money. What was it that Avis told the public? "We are Avis; we *try harder!*"

When you are wanting to be number one, and the position is already filled, so the best you can be is number two, the only thing left for you to do is try harder. There is something in all of us that cheers on the underdog. People began to support Avis because they were "trying harder." These days, there are so many rental-car companies to choose from that the market share is divided up a lot more thinly than it was in the sixties. But for a while there, Avis became the only competition for the number-one position, and for a season they really outdid their competitor.

I don't care who you are or how gifted you are, it seems that the pressure to perform can get to you regardless.

Competition can be quite unhealthy when it turns ugly, as in the case of Jacob and Esau; however, being competitive can serve a greater purpose. It often can bring out the stuff you are really made of and give you the guts to go for the gold.

Jacob tried harder. The contest with his brother taught him how to survive and persist, which would serve him well later on in life. Yet had he only seen that his brother struggled to maintain that number-one position, he might have been a bit more compassionate and understanding.

For all of Esau's bravado, he returned home from one of his adventures in the wild exhausted and empty. Esau lived for the field. The wild place was in his heart; the untamed place was his territory. While the gift naturally flowed out of him to hunt his prey and conquer the unknown, the pressure to perform for his dad's approval was as much there for him as it was for Jacob. I don't care who you are or how gifted you are, it seems that the pressure to perform can get to you regardless.

If you have to work for your approval, then what kind of approval is it, really? For sure, it isn't unconditional approval. It's approval based on how well you perform. Even Esau felt that pressure. Oh, he may not have felt it when everything was going well. However, have a day or two in the field where nothing went his way, and he, too, became weary to the point of exhaustion and even discouragement.

Here comes the number-one hunter of the family, home from the field after long hours, empty-handed. He had nothing to show his father, nothing to fill his hands, and nothing to fill his stomach. He wasn't even concerned now about filling his dad's stomach; it was his own appetite that mattered more than anything.

Interestingly enough, his tent-dwelling, lentil-cooking, peace loving brother was calmly sitting at home cooking up some stew from the lentils he grew in their backyard. No great effort on his part to have to go far to get something to satisfy his appetite. While his brother was out there in the intense heat of the wilderness hunting wild beasts, Jacob was cultivating the soil of his garden, planting rows of lentil seeds, and watering his crops. Once they came to maturity, he would calmly walk through the garden, gather his harvest in bushels, and take it into the tent to clean it, soak it, and prepare it for consumption.

It didn't seem like much of an adventurous life to Esau. As a matter of fact, Jacob's whole existence seemed a bore to his brother. Esau probably wondered how in the world such a mild-mannered mama's boy could ever hope to be considered for the number-one position with his dad. He was anything but the image of perfection.

You know, though, when you are weary and concerned only about survival, you find that even the thing you find least tasty, and the person you have the most distaste for in your life, has something you desperately need. Esau needed his brother. How ironic this is! It is amazing to me that when it comes to survival, the people we avoid at all costs sometimes have the very thing we need. At some level, Jacob knew his brother needed him. Esau was so consumed with satisfying the pangs of hunger in his belly that he was oblivious to the strategy his brother came up with right there on the spot. Ah yes, *there* was that moment!

As difficult as it is to deal with Jacob's motives, one thing seems clear: for the first time in his life, it dawned on Jacob that he had something that—even if only for a moment—was valued by his older brother. That touched something at the core of Jacob. Yet it also stirred up the determination to take advantage of the situation for the sake of what mattered most to him: the birthright. That is the thing Jacob couldn't let go of, and for the first time in his life, he felt it was within his reach.

Donald Trump would give Jacob high marks for his shrewdness and wise business sense in this transaction. Jacob had something his brother needed. That is a power position, isn't it? Jacob would use that position of power, though it wasn't just power he was after. He had his eyes on the greater prize: the right of the firstborn son to be heir to the family inheritance to the tune of double what his brother would get. It wasn't just the riches of Isaac; it was a place in history as the inheritor of the legacy of Abraham and the promise of the seed that would bless every family on earth. The stakes were high.

Esau watched as Jacob stirred up the pot and released the aroma of that lentil stew. With every rotation of the spoon, he was also stirring the appetite of his brother. He had a hold on him, and he wasn't letting go. "If you are really hungry for what I have," Jacob suggested, "then give me what I want!"

"What's that?" retorted Esau.

"Before I put one spoonful of this stew on your plate, which matters so much to you that you'll give up anything, then once and for all give up the birthright and sell it to me in exchange for the soup," was Jacob's reply. You have to give Jacob credit for a few things. He was determined. And he also really did want to be included in the covenant history of the promise to his grandfather from God Himself. He had an eye for what the birthright meant to his family, his future, and his father.

Unfortunately for Esau, he didn't place all that much value on the birthright. He was willing to let it go for some soup. He believed he was going to die if he didn't get it all now. He was seeking to save his life for himself, not realizing that in so doing he would actually lose it *and* his place in the grand scheme of things. That is like being willing to give up a miracle of healing from emphysema for just one more cigarette. Sad as it is, I have seen one too many make that same kind of choice. They could have chosen long life, yet they chose to satisfy their appetites for the moment one more time, and they ended up losing everything.

Jacob was shrewd, he was clever, and yet he was far from loving and compassionate. Esau was driven and desperate and far from valuing what mattered most. The two of them were both clawing for something. They both wanted it all—right then and there. In actual fact they both got more than they bargained for.

HAVING IT ALL

You really can have it all; you just can't have it all right now. When you can't let go of your need to have it all now, you invite more pain into your life in your future, where unexpected things are waiting for you based on the choices you have made.

For all his incredible talent, rock music's Jimi Hendrix sold his birthright for a mess of drug "stew." So did Janis Joplin, Jim Morrison, and many others. The same story can be told about more recent icons like Curt Kobain. How do you go from a band called Nirvana, which means "bliss" or "heaven," to a place of self-destruction? These all had promising futures, they all had painful pasts, and they were all hoping their performance would be good enough to get them the approval they desperately longed for. It wasn't okay to let go. It wasn't safe to let go.

You have to wonder if they ever really valued their birthrights. In actual fact, was it ever really okay for them to be who they were? They didn't live long enough to even find out.

Whether we are discussing the counterculture of the sixties, the challenge that the youth of the new millennium are facing, or Jacob and Esau's grabbing for something that each knew the other had, at the core we are all wrestling with the same issues: believing we are supposed to have it all and demanding to have it *now!* You can't, I can't, and we can't, but we do our best to convince ourselves that we can.

But there is One who watches, evaluates, and directs without our knowing it, and He uses it all to bring us to a place where we are willing to face the parts of us that scare us the most. Only when we get to that place will we ever stop fighting everyone else and realize we are fighting ourselves. Only when that One brings us to that moment of truth can we really have it all.

CHAPTER 5 | WHEN YOU CAN'T LET GO OF THE FEAR OF NOT BEING AROUND ANYMORE

Now it came about, when Isaac was old, and his eyes were too dim to see, that he called his older son Esau and said to him, "My son." And he said to him, "Here I am." And Isaac said, "Behold now, I am old and I do not know the day of my death. Now then, please take your gear, your quiver and your bow, and go out to the field and hunt game for me; and prepare a savory dish for me such as I love, and bring it to me that I may eat, so that my soul may bless you before I die." And Rebekah was listening while Isaac spoke to his son Esau.
—Genesis 27:1–5 NASB

If you read between the lines, Rebekah constantly had to keep an eye on Isaac, because he was losing his vision. But vision is far more than sight.

Isaac had clearly ignored the clear indication from the God of his father, Abraham, that the younger of the two boys would be the heir apparent to the blessing and birthright. The Lord had already spoken it while Rebekah was pregnant:

"Two nations are in your womb,
Two peoples shall be separated from your body;
One people shall be stronger than the other,
And the OLDER shall serve the YOUNGER."
(Genesis 25:23, emphasis mine)

This revelation apparently mattered little to Isaac. He obviously refused to accept whatever it meant and rejected the idea altogether that God meant for Jacob to have the birthright. What else can you conclude based on Isaac's behavior at this point?

Look carefully at the text and you see that Isaac was first and foremost interested in satisfying his own appetite. When his belly was filled, then he would find the energy to release his soul's blessing to his older son. It was all about Isaac. He was a tough nut to crack. He was stubborn and obstinate and wouldn't let go of what *he* wanted.

It is vitally important to value the intention and design of God in your life, even if at times it doesn't make sense to you. It really takes a whole lot of trust and faith to pray the prayer "Not my will, but Thy will be done." Some consider that a prayer of fatalism. But the One who prayed it didn't think it was. In actuality, for Him it was an acknowledgment of surrender to the highest good of others and the ultimate best for Himself because He trusted in the imminent goodness of the One He called "Father."

The God who is always good is able to reveal Himself in all

His goodness to you in the midst of every conflict and every decision. It does, however, take simple childlike trust for that to happen. The only other option is to hold on tight to unworthy suspicions and skepticism about His goodness. Isaac evidently had robbers in his own inner temple and refused to drive them out.

Conflicts and decisions are part of what perfect your vision and your perceptions of reality, provided you choose appropriately. Anyone who wants to tell you there is an easy way to genuine self-control and self-mastery in the achievement of your highest purpose is not speaking from experience or from truth. It is a series of choices from beginning to end, some of them difficult. If you choose based on satisfying your appetite instead of honoring a timeless principle, it will cost you more than you bargained for in the end. You are ultimately responsible for everything you think, say, do, and feel!

Yielding to a Power greater than you and Wisdom beyond yourself takes humility. Yet in the yielding there comes a gift of great peace and the grace to *see* the goodness of God. But while Isaac was still in the land of the living, he couldn't see a thing except the need to satisfy his taste for something wild.

It is a tragic thing indeed to come to the end of your life and miss the real purpose for which you were created. By the time you've lived through as much as Isaac had, and managed the number of crucial transitions that he did to be in a place where God can bring about your future through His promise, you would think that wisdom would prevail. Sadly, it doesn't always prevail. The old "have it your way" motto of Burger King is not necessarily going to get you the life of your dreams. It may actually blind you to the larger picture of the legacy you can leave behind for others.

Poor old Isaac could not trust the unknown. He could not have faith in what he could not control. This one, who in his youth climbed up a mountain to be a willing sacrifice in utter trust of his father and his goodness, had lost his childlike ability to surrender to what he could not be in command of, namely, Jacob's handling of the inheritance. The fear of death brings with it a fear of nonbeing. Isaac believed he wouldn't "be" anymore. That is the great fear and the great lie of which the powers of darkness have convinced the masses of humanity for millennia. If anyone should have known that God is not the God of the dead, but of the living, it should have been Isaac! Yet Isaac was afraid that his identity would be forever eliminated, and he couldn't stand it.

The old "have it your way" motto of Burger King is not necessarily going to get you the life of your dreams.

When life is hounded by death, and you realize that you are about to detach from so many things that were once important, other things take on deeper significance for you. Making amends with loved ones that have never heard you say, "I love you" is one of the more common things I have personally witnessed when called to the bedside of a dying person. Isaac wanted to make peace, yet he wanted to make it on *his* terms, not on God's terms. He refused to let go of Esau.

Isaac was going through his final identity crisis. He knew he was quite old. He also knew his vision was getting dimmer by the minute. His bodily functions seemed to be shutting down, and he could feel life slipping away. Do you want to know what Isaac's identity crisis really was? His identity crisis was simply what American psychoanalyst Erik Erikson declared regarding this major transition in life called death: "I am what survives me." So what would survive Isaac? What did he want his legacy to be? He wanted it to be the wild, untamed son who could not be held back from the hunt for prey. He wanted Esau to be his identity that survived his death.

Isaac had so hardened himself against what really needed to take place that he not only could not see the truth, but he had lost his ability to hear it. For all the incredible things Isaac did in his life, he failed to honor his ultimate purpose: to pass on the birthright to the unloved son, Jacob.

It just so happened that when he called to his son Esau and invited him into the tent, Rebekah's ears were wide open. She had never stopped remembering what she had heard, perhaps decades earlier, during her difficult pregnancy. God had opened her heart and let her know that the younger and weaker of the two was to be the rightful heir to the birthright and blessing. Somebody in the family had to honor the greater wisdom that came as a gift of grace during the night season. If Isaac would fail to honor what God had said, it would fall to Rebekah.

God had Rebekah in the right place at the right time to intercept a message that, had she not been there, would have altered history forever.

CHAPTER 6 | WHEN YOU CAN'T LET GO OF BEING THE PERSON YOU WERE NEVER BORN TO BE

"Prepare a savory dish for me such as I love, and bring it to me that I may eat, so that my soul may bless you before I die."
—Genesis 27:4 NASB

Esau was commissioned by his father to go out and produce/perform for his dad one last time, and to feed his father's taste for the wild things. But Rebekah just happened to be right outside of the line of sight of both Esau and her all-too-blind husband, Isaac. She intercepted a message that she was not supposed to be privy to, and immediately summoned her stew-cooking son, Jacob.

Rebekah made it clear to Jacob that he was to go get the finest of the kids from the flock and bring them to her so she could prepare a meal that would be every bit as tasty as Esau's meal was going to be. Strange, isn't it, that Jacob was a chef in his own right, yet his mother couldn't trust him to make a meal that would pass muster with Isaac? Jacob's competence for cooking up the kind of stuff that would satisfy his father obviously fell short. But Rebekah, more than anyone, knew what satisfied Isaac's taste buds. Her intent was to act quickly and feed Isaac long before Esau could get home—and before Isaac realized what was going on.

Rebekah would send Jacob into the tent of his blind father, pretending to be Esau. He would then present to Isaac a meal that he could not even produce on his own, because he wasn't gifted to do so. Yet he was expected to go in and act as if he really did catch, clean, cook, and serve the meal, without even breaking a sweat.

When Mom made known the plan to her younger son, he struggled, because he knew he could not perform like his brother. He would be going in under false pretenses to receive a blessing for something he did not and could not produce. He would be going into the tent based on the performance of someone else. This was not a comfortable position to be in.

If that weren't enough, he also knew that he didn't look or even smell like his brother. They were twins, yet they were far from identical. Esau was covered in hair from top to bottom. Jacob didn't even have enough hair growing on his face to have a moustache. And he was fair skinned.

Falling prey to the performance trap is so common in life. If you can just perform "up to par" and live up to someone else's expectations, everything will be just fine. Right? Unfortunately, sometimes the harder you try, the harder others are to please. You will always end up being someone else and not yourself.

Being Esau came naturally for Esau. It did not come naturally for Jacob. You can't be someone else no matter how hard you try. In the peak-performance business, which has to do with when you are at the top of your game, there is a phrase known as "unconscious competence." It simply means that you have this incredible ability to perform without having to give your performance a second thought. Actually, you don't even have to give it a first thought, because you are simply flowing at your peak out of who you truly are at your core.

Unfortunately, sometimes the harder you try, the harder others are to please. You will always end up being someone else and not yourself.

What Tiger Woods makes look so incredibly easy as a pro golfer is virtually impossible for someone who hasn't got the swing of things in golf. Tiger made it look easy even when he was only two years old and appeared on the *Mike Douglas Show*. Tiger was created for golf (and if you talk to some overzealous Tiger fans, they might even say golf was created for Tiger). He flows in his uniqueness from the inside out. He is comfortable with who he is, what he can do, and what he can obtain as a result.

Michael Jordan in his heyday on the basketball courts was the same way. He made those three-pointers look so easy. It was simply a part of who he was. There was a grace, a flow, an economy of movement that was an expression of his "unconscious competence." Coming down court and doing a twist in the air, rolling the ball down one arm, off his fingertips, and through the hoop in a fly-through-the-air layup was too incredible to reproduce by anyone. This is the artistry that comes from a deep place in one's core. This is unconscious competence, and it simply flows from who a person is.

When you are Michael Jordan, that's all you have to be. When you're Tiger Woods, you simply have to be yourself, and the rest will follow suit. Copy Tiger's style all you want, but you will never *be* Tiger. Imitate Michael's moves if you dare, but sooner or later you will discover you have to simply be yourself when you face the crisis of your own identity.

If you are like Esau, you are good at your "game." You simply hunt it down, outsmart it, trap it, take it home, prepare it, and offer it as the fruit of your peak performance.

But if you are Jacob, and it isn't really okay to be Jacob (especially in the eyes of Isaac), no matter how hard you try to perform, you cannot achieve unconscious competence in Esau's gift. It simply isn't who you are. The harder you try, the worse it will get. You are unconsciously competent, but it is in a different area, and it will take a different environment to bring it out of you. Jacob's moment to shine would come later on, at another time, in another place; however, there was really no other way for him to get to where he was going than to experience what he had to experience for himself.

Like it or not, there are some things that are part of a pathway toward becoming who we truly are. It isn't fate I am talking about; it is the path of wisdom from the Source of all wisdom. The only way out of this crisis is to go through it.

Jacob's drama was unfolding here for the entire world to see for generations to come. Whether we like the way the story reads or not, this is the way it was. So many people have gone back to this story and second-guessed the way it "should" have happened. Well, life doesn't work that way, and God is big enough to use it all for the ultimate best whether we speculate about "what coulda, woulda, or shoulda" happened. Therapist and author Virginia Satir said, "Life is not the way it's supposed to be. It is the way it is. The way you cope with it is what makes the difference."

Jacob was facing this crisis, and it was of no small proportions. In the Chinese language the word *crisis* is composed of two characters that are placed together. One means "danger," and the other means "opportunity." When you put it all together, the word in Chinese implies a *dangerous opportunity*. This was for sure a dangerous opportunity for Jacob. He would have to either be himself in total transparency, or appear to be the person he least wanted to be (and would *never* be, no matter how hard he tried). Jacob really believed he needed to be Esau in order to obtain what he longed for, and unless he could find it out for himself, all the talk to the contrary was useless.

Some lessons in life can only be learned by personal experience. The need to find out for yourself what fits and what doesn't, what works and what doesn't, is rarely something you will find in a textbook. Oh, if only your choices could be made for you, life would be so easy . . . yet it wouldn't be life; it would be a form of robotic animation. You would be programmed to respond in specific ways, and you would lose touch with genuine human experience in all its rich texture, combining the joys and sorrows, the ups and the downs, and the opportunities as well as the adversities that make up the rich resources of your personal history. Yes, even your pain becomes a rich resource and a gift when you discover what it means to have learned something from it.

> Therapist and author Virginia Satir said, "Life is not the way it's supposed to be. It is the way it is. The way you cope with it is what makes the difference."

Letting go of who you thought you were supposed to be to become who you really are doesn't happen all at once. It takes time, and time involves embracing a process.

FITTING THE MOLD

All too often you have been forced to squeeze into a mold that wasn't made for you. If you hated trigonometry—even though you were told that graduation from high school was impossible without it—you still had to take it. Unless you are an architect, how many times have you needed to know about the attributes of an isosceles triangle? Yet you were squeezed into that mold for a time, even if you passed trig by the skin of your teeth.

At one time in the late 1800s, it was fashionable for women to force their feet into shoes that were too small, as women were "supposed to have" small feet. They also had to wear corsets that practically suffocated them, just to appear to have the perfect shape. Ask the poor soul who attempted to squeeze a size 7 foot into a size 5 shoe if it made walking more natural and comfortable. Ask any woman who has ever worn a corset if it was worth the pain. And what earthly wisdom dictated that a woman be squeezed into such a mold from top to bottom? Madison Avenue!

The Europeans had Paris to set the trends for fashion, and New York was becoming the fashion center for America. And if Madison Avenue said this is the way it was, then you had to fit in, of course, even if it killed you! Well, what person feeling the pressure of media hype and bombardment long enough wants to be left out? Who really starts out wanting to be different? We tend to want to fit in and belong.

How many infomercials have mesmerized you into buying the latest piece of exercise equipment to give you that perfect shape? How many fad diets have you tried in order to lose those inches? The underlying media message is simply this: it *isn't* okay to be who you are; you have to be somebody else that is really perfect. Ever listen to interviews with some of the so-called "perfect people" that everyone worships because they are superstars? Ever hear the pain that many of them have endured when the bright lights and cameras weren't pointed at them? They have had far-from-perfect lives. Many have even wished they could trade places with you! Imagine that.

Discovering the truth that what is appropriate for someone

else may not be appropriate for you takes time; sometimes it takes a long time. When you bury your feelings and hope they will go away, you are burying a part of you that is crying out. Bury it deep enough, and it slips into the recesses of your heart and drives you without your conscious awareness.

The underlying media message is simply this: it isn't okay to be who you are; you have to be somebody else that is really perfect.

If you are driven to get acceptance no matter what price you have to pay, you will learn the hard way that it just doesn't pay to be someone other than yourself. J. B. Phillips in *The New Testament in Modern English* translates Paul's words this way: "Don't let the world around you squeeze you into its own mould" (Romans 12:2).

When you are raised in an environment in which you are told that the world works only a certain way, it is difficult to believe that life can be different. If you had been told by everyone in authority that the world was flat and that if you got too close to the edge you would fall off, it wouldn't have been popular to be Christopher Columbus. He had to choose his destination rather carefully in the midst of a hostile group of religious "experts" who basically convinced the whole world that what they said was absolute.

I wonder how long it took for Columbus to find a crew that was willing to not only believe in the possibility of a round world, but to actually set sail on that new and round world, trust their compass, and sail toward the "edge." Columbus had to let go and become who he truly was. It cost him something. He had to face a crisis. It probably took a lot more time than history books tell us in a few paragraphs, to find others who were willing to take the journey away from the molds they had been squeezed into.

VALUE JUDGMENTS

Jacob had to go on this journey. Like it or not, this was a moment of truth, albeit painful truth. He was about to find out what it was like to be his brother and to get close enough to his father for a moment of father-son intimacy.

Let's suppose that intimacy means "into-me scc." Jacob wanted "into-me-see" experiences with his dad. He had never had them. He deeply yearned for them more than anything else. Perhaps, as painful as it was, playing the part of Esau would give him that experience. Or perhaps it would only heighten his fear of rejection and the pain of not being good enough.

Jacob had no desire to deceive his father, and he fought his mother's request tooth and nail. He resisted her suggestion for fear he would be regarded as a deceiver in his father's eyes, blind as those eyes already were. Isn't it interesting that the younger son, whom so many had already labeled a deceiver, really had no desire to mislead his father? The guy was torn up inside. All he ever wanted was his dad's approval.

The pain inside Jacob was almost too great to bear. He wanted the blessing that went along with the birthright; he just didn't want it this way. By the way, this stuff isn't exclusive to fathers and sons. It can happen with mothers and sons, fathers and daughters, mothers and daughters, teachers and students, or any other combination you might come up with where one deeply wants approval and acceptance from someone he or she looks up to.

Jacob's greatest fear was that he would bring a curse upon himself. If he was found out as a deceiver, his father had the power to curse the remainder of Jacob's life, and he came from a long line of folk that lived for hundreds of years! There was a whole lot at stake.

Death and life, after all, are in the power of the tongue (Proverbs 18:21). Words can either create life or destroy life depending on who is uttering them and how much influence these individuals have in your life. The more significant the authority figure, and the more you look up to that figure, the more detrimental his or her negative words can be.

Jacob lived in a world of punishment, conflict, war at the heels of his brother, competition, win-lose relationships, fear-based decisions, and worst-case scenarios. That is certainly not a world of total unconditional acceptance. It is far from a world of peace and hope. It is a world guaranteed to further your pain and frustration. Ever met anybody who lived there? Ever wish you could help him or her (or yourself for that matter) find a way to let go and finally be who he or she really is?

Jacob was caught in a crisis, a moment of decision, a moment of danger as well as opportunity. Rebekah took full responsibility and told her son that the curse would be hers to bear, not his; his responsibility was to obey her and to trust her in the matter (Genesis 27:13). While many condemn Rebekah and Jacob here for being deceptive, the fact remains that Rebekah was acting out of obedience to the clear intention of God. There was no other way around this difficult situation. A careful look at all the evidence and you will discover that Rebekah was God's instrument for recovery, and Jacob was bound to obey her voice. Rebekah was bound by a higher law and knew that her strategy was the only way to fulfillment, at least based on the light she had at that season of her life.

I have learned a hard lesson in life, both in my own experience and in observing the experience of others: You can play the if-I-could-live-my-life-over game, but it won't really accomplish much that is healthy, positive, and affirming. The truth is, if you had the chance to do it all over again, you would make the same decisions you did the first time. Why? At the time you made the decision, you used the resources and information that were available to you and the insight you had at that season of your life. You did the best you could with what you had. Most people do.

It is much more psychologically sound to acknowledge where you have been and accept that you did the best you could with what you had. Even if a part of you isn't totally convinced, it is still a much healthier way of moving through life, sorting out your personal history, and embracing your destiny.

> The truth is, if you had the chance to do it all over again, you would make the same decisions you did the first time.

Isaac was determined to act in accordance with his own desires. He was going to bless Esau *no matter what*. But in his culture and society, once a declaration was uttered, it was final! Once the blessing went out of his mouth, it could not be taken back. So even if Isaac indeed blessed Jacob while attempting to bless Esau, that blessing could not be revoked. The declaration would be sealed for good.

It is also important to know that once the birthright was sold to Jacob, it was a legal transaction. Once the transaction was completed, there could be no reversal of it, either; it would be as binding as the declaration of the family blessing.

Here is the naked truth: Esau sold the birthright to his younger brother because it had no lasting value to him. Years later, the prophet Malachi would declare that God loved Jacob for honoring and seeing the value in the birthright, and that God despised Esau for dishonoring it (1:2–3). If you were to play the role of attorney for the defense that Jacob was innocent of the accusation of religious leaders throughout the centuries, and that Rebekah was also innocent of all charges leveled against her, your first witness might have to be a hostile witness: Esau.

Esau would be the first one to level the accusation against his brother that he was a "supplanter." Religious leaders would follow suit and take up his case for millennia. This case needs to be reopened. In the Hebrew, many words have double meanings. The play on words here is revealing. The double meaning of "Jacob" is both "heel grabber" and "supplanter." One is simply a description of an external behavior. The other is a value judgment of an inner condition and motive. The word *supplanter* is *never* used as a label against Jacob until his angry and resentful brother Esau comes in from the hunt and finds his brother has obtained the blessing from Isaac. At that point, Esau chooses to use the double meaning of the name "heel grabber," and with hatred and resentment projects his anger onto Jacob by calling him a supplanter (Genesis 27:36).

When you are judgmental, you are in violation of the law of love. All value judging is a projection of your own unfinished business. You cannot judge in someone else what you have not first judged in your own heart.

When you cannot simply accept the reality of situations, people, events, or whatever, and let them be what they are, you impose your judgments on them. At that point you cannot offer them unconditional acceptance, because you are not living in it yourself. The only way to experience total unconditional acceptance is to *let go* of the drive to value judge. Easier said than done, you say? Of course it is; most of the time you and I aren't even conscious that we are doing it. So how do we know we are value judging? It really is simple: we feel uncomfortable inside. We have not only passed judgment on the other person when we pointed the finger at his or her motives, but we also passed judgment on ourselves. We played God and suffered our own condemnation. Or how about when you go through a crisis and you name it "the worst thing that ever happened in my life"? That, my dear friend, is also a value judgment. Judge it the worst thing that ever happened, and you will build a strong case for proving it in your experience.

When you pass judgment on others, your judgments don't just diminish them, but they also fuel the self-talk that diminishes you! Until you learn how to let go and refuse to embrace criticism, sarcasm, comparison, and the like, you'll keep attracting the most nonaffirming things into your life.

We live in a day and age when so many people claim to follow the teachings of Jesus, and yet they continually hold on to the very thing He insisted they let go of. He said, "Judge not, that you be not judged" (Matthew 7:1). Sadly, we live unconscious lives, asleep in the light, and give lip service to the incredible wisdom that came from the Nazarene Carpenter's mouth. And yet we behave exactly opposite His instruction. To top it all off, we then boldly proclaim our allegiance to Him. It's pretty scary stuff, don't you think?

How often have you heard someone cry out against a stranger's inappropriate behavior, and then that person's own child, grandchild, or loved one falls into the same trap? All of a sudden, when your family experiences the pain of abortion or something similar, you have to work through the family dynamics that may have created a portion of the pain. Granted, that example is an extreme one, yet it isn't unknown, at least in the course of my life in the people-helping business.

I recall a woman who spoke out openly, condemning teenage girls for getting pregnant out of wedlock—then it happened to her daughter. It was a bitter pill to swallow. The hard-nosed approach to the letter of the law can prevent a person from accepting and loving the life that comes from the womb. That dear lady had to make a decision to let go of who she thought she was and become who she was meant to be for her sake, her daughter's sake, *and* the sake of her new grandchild.

Big or small, value judging is a projection of our own unfinished business, and often it shows our failure to face the real issues in our own hearts. The "heel grabber" bought the birthright from Esau fair and square. There was no love lost between them, and Esau had no sense of value for the intention of God in the birthright, or for values that were bigger than his appetite.

SEEING THE TRUTH

Now that it is time to get the benefits of the birthright, Esau is a day late and a dollar short. He is angry with Jacob for taking what was already his. He is angry with his father for being blind to it all. The real issue that he fails to recognize is his own self-hatred and how he projects that onto his brother.

Esau gives emphasis to the double meaning of *supplanter*, while Jacob is simply someone who grabbed his brother's heel at birth. The venomous twist in the name *Jacob* comes from the lips of a hateful brother who had a need to justify his own failure to honor something. He didn't see his birthright's value when he sold it, so why should he deserve its power when it's time to be passed on?

After Isaac had blessed the "wrong" son (so much for seeing the truth), Esau came in from the hunt. In shock, Isaac then fed Esau's already-simmering anger and said to him, "Your brother came with deceit and has taken away your blessing" (Genesis 27:35). Is that really what happened? Why didn't Isaac take any responsibility here for dishonoring the legal transaction between the two sons and the divine revelation that came at birth? This is the human condition in all its nakedness. Esau spewed out his bitterness by saying, "Is he not rightly named Jacob? For he has *supplanted* me these two times. He *took away* my birthright [notice Esau contending that he didn't sell it freely], and now look, he has taken away my blessing!" (v. 36). The difficulty for both Esau and Isaac in this entire ordeal is that the ultimate decision involved an unfolding series of choices that they made against the truth from the outset. Paul says in 2 Corinthians 13:8, "We can do nothing against the truth, but for the truth."

It is a sad situation for Isaac and Esau; however, there are larger issues at play here, and pity offers little power for them to be transformed beyond their limited vision. You will either embrace the truth in your life or be forced to prove it when you resist it. Whatever you resist will persist, and ultimately all resistance is inside you, though you and I want to believe it is in our circumstances or something outside of us.

> You will either embrace the truth in your life or be forced to prove it when you resist it.

This doesn't, however, let Jacob off the hook for his behavior or its consequences. Neither does it make the situation any easier for him when he enters the tent in the name of his brother Esau, which we will explore in the next chapter.

HONORING THE MESSAGE

A wise Man once said, "Take care what you listen to. By your standard of measure it shall be measured to you; and more shall be given you besides. For whoever has, to him shall more be given; and whoever does not have, even what he has shall be taken away from him" (Mark 4:24–25 NASB). Isaac knew as well as Rebekah what God had said while the twins were yet in their mother's womb. He had the opportunity from the outset to honor what God made clear. The ancients were far more aware of direct experiences with God than many people are today. Rebekah knew that she had been given a direct word from the Almighty. Isaac actually knew it too! But he still chose to ignore the message.

Isaac was imprisoned by the need to be in control and seemed to have the idea that he was entitled to have it all his way. He chose to squeeze God's big picture into his limited understanding and make it fit his own concept of how things should work out. He was too blind to identify the point from which he was viewing his life, his sons' lives, and the intention and wisdom of God. The result was that there was no room to build an altar to the wisdom of God like his dad, Abraham, had built. Altars for you and me are places in our hearts and minds where we build benchmarks for real knowledge and growth.

POINT OF VIEW

By the time Isaac came of age, he had experienced firsthand the possibility of losing his life at the hands of his father. He was with Abraham in his crisis of faith in the land of Moriah (see Genesis 22:2). That had to be a difficult thing for the young man, wouldn't you say? Isaac willingly carried the wood for the burnt offering up a mountain alongside his father. That much we know. What we don't know is what he was sorting out on the inside when he realized he was the one being sacrificed.

He saw his father build an altar and arrange that circle of stones where the sacrifice would be laid, drawn and quartered, and burned as a gift to God. Then his father took him by the hand, laid him on top of the stones and the wood, and bound him to the altar of sacrifice. Isaac was like a lamb led to the slaughter, and he didn't even open his mouth. But what was going on in his heart?

Wasn't he as human as you or me? Didn't he possibly feel quite vulnerable at that moment, and perhaps even confused that someone who loved him so much could also be willing to sacrifice him? At least his brother, Ishmael, had been given a fighting chance to go it alone in the desert. But Isaac couldn't run from this moment if he tried. Abraham had given God an unconditional yes. He arrived at a place where he refused to be squeezed into a limiting mold that would diminish his ability to have all that God wanted him to have. His altar would serve as a benchmark for really knowing the heart and intent of God and His desire to not withhold any good thing from Abraham.

Isaac may have outwardly been willing; however, it would seem that his "yes" to his father was conditional, and as a result, his "yes" to God was also conditional. Isaac may have looked as though he was really willing to die, but given his behavior with Jacob and Esau, I would venture to say that he couldn't stand the fact that death was about to get the best of him. Permanence beyond death is only possible when God's life is at work in the situation. Isaac never benchmarked that experience deep in his soul in a way that caused him to give up his limited point of view.

God never intended to allow Abraham to slaughter Isaac, though some seem to connect the pagan practices of his day to his actions on the mount with Isaac. The pagans of Abraham's day did offer their children as sacrifices to the gods of their superstitions. So when Isaac saw his father lift that knife, he had to feel the intense pressure of knowing he was about to lose his life.

> Permanence beyond death is only possible when
> God's life is at work in the situation.

All of a sudden, the heavens opened and Isaac heard the Angel stay the hand of his father. And as God spoke with Abraham, Isaac was part of a critical moment of history and saw a life larger than the present moment!

Then Isaac saw a ram, which had come up the other side of Mount Moriah, caught by its horns in a bush of thorns. Something that was as wild and untamed as Ishmael and Esau was caught in a thicket. Maybe there was a ramlike nature in Abraham that had refused to be tamed that was finally caught too.

How often does it take a willingness to climb up a mountain called Moriah, which can be interpreted, "God is my teacher," where God shows us what we can't see from our limited point of view? While we are trusting that it will all work out well and making the climb to lay everything down that could hold us back from our ultimate best, up the other side of the mountain comes a beast that portrays the part of us that has to have its own way and refuses to be transformed. What force caused that ram to come up the unseen side of that mountain? The trust and surrender of Abraham, who, like that ram, finally let go of doing things the way they had always been done.

When you surrender your ramlike determination and trust to a Power greater than yourself, that ramlike thinking gets caught in the thorns.

When Abraham and Isaac saw that ram, they knew something had shifted, and both experienced a level of real transformation. Your struggle to be free from the predictable and limiting mold that others want to keep you in has the power to transform you!

HEEL GRABBERS

When we all get to heaven, I am convinced there will be a long line of theologians and preachers waiting to beg forgiveness of a man they misrepresented for centuries in all of their sermons. Behind them will be a host of people who believed what those preachers said and also passed judgment on the younger son of Isaac, whom God loved and favored.

If God loved Jacob, you and I need to love him too. There are sound and healthy reasons for doing so. There is a Jacob inside of *you*, a heel grabber that was destined to reach for inheritance. God can work with all those parts of you that don't quite measure up.

There is a reason that the sacred text calls God the "God of Jacob" more than any other title He is given. That at least tells you that God does favor the one who is the underdog. Heel grabbers that are born reaching for the highest, brightest, and best of God's intentions get help all along the way to become who they truly are. It's only the folk that live for their appetites that lose everything for the sake of temporary satisfaction.

When what matters most to you is what you were created and designed for, the smile of God will be there all the time, in spite of all the things that are stacked against you. *Eventually you will learn, through many dangers and strange pathways, that it is safe to let go—but not until you grab hold of the heel of the One who made you to be who you are!*

CHAPTER 7 | WHEN YOU CAN'T LET GO OF THE MASK THAT HIDES THE REAL YOU

So [Jacob] went to his father and said, "My father." And he said, "Here I am. Who are you my son?" Jacob said to his father, "I am Esau your firstborn."—Genesis 27:18–19

Jim Carrey, in the comedy *The Mask*, plays a weak character named Stanley Ipkiss, who finds a mysterious tribal mask of a Norse god that transforms him into a manic superhero. The challenge is that once he puts the mask on, it is really hard to take off. *The Mask* is slapstick comedy at its worst, or perhaps its best, depending on who is watching the movie. The irony of it all is how often *we* mask *our* true identities because there is a more appealing kind of role we prefer.

The truth is that the whole of life is marked by seasons of stability as well as crisis. There are seasons when adults are really excited about who they are, and at other times they are in crisis over their roles. Sometimes you can go through turbulent seasons in your life because who you have been no longer serves to help you become who you desire to be. Answering the question, *Who are you?* isn't as easy as it may seem.

How do you know who you really are? You grow up in a world where, from the time you are little, you are expected to fulfill certain roles. You have to be child, student, son or daughter, foster child, adoptee, or whatever. You are shaped in part not only by what you feel from a deep place inside, but also by what is directing you from the outside: parental expectations, peer pressure, environment, and culture. Usually you don't get to pick your boundaries in your formative years; they are picked for you.

It isn't until you leave the nest, get out on your own, and do "your thing" that you begin to test those boundaries in order to find out what does or doesn't fit in your life, who you are, and, most importantly, who you are not. The truth is that those issues don't come to the surface until we are just about ready to leave home or have left home.

Some people never leave home, others wait until they find someone to marry, and others venture out the moment they are "legal" in their state. In all my years of dealing with people, I haven't met too many that haven't tried to prove they weren't a Xerox of Mom and Dad. It seems that most people that finally leave home have as their first task to disassociate from being just like Mom and Dad.

But it takes a lot more to leave home than simply getting an apartment, a job or a career, or a spouse. There are deep patterns that have been engrained in your very being. You take "home" with you whether you want to or not. Your home environment has taken up residence inside you. You bring that environment, that heredity, and all that history with you, and all of that can at times fight hard against the part of you that intuitively believes that there is more to you than meets the eye. There is a part of you that also may discover that there is more to you than the many masks you wear.

> There are deep patterns that have been engrained in your very being. You take "home" with you whether you want to or not.

Jacob has come of age, or at least it seems as if he is being forced to come of age. Isaac is convinced he doesn't have all that many years left to live. He has lost his vision and, as a result, has lost his mobility. He stays preoccupied with his appetite and his impending death. Sadly, when you do a careful study of how long Isaac lived after he pronounced the blessing of the birthright on Jacob, he actually had another eighty years left! How limited was his vision?

Isaac's determination to preempt the wisdom and purpose of God is about to force Jacob into a season of deep instability and crisis. This is for sure a dangerous opportunity. Life as Jacob has known it while growing up is about to come to an end.

Jacob's mother takes the skins and the rough hair of the goats from the flock and does a quick tanning and dry-cleaning job on them, then pastes them onto Jacob's hands and chest. He is being dressed up to look and even *smell* like his brother, Esau. Like Stanley Ipkiss, Jim Carrey's character, Jacob is about to mask his true identity in order to get something he wants more than anything else. It just doesn't dawn on him how high the price will be for wearing the "mask."

Jacob enters the tent. If ever the mask will get him what he wants, this is the moment. He feels insecure, inadequate, and uncertain about himself, as though he has no identity. He is in a position of weakness, not power.

He doesn't just bring with him a disguise; he brings the whole background of his family environment with all its unfinished business into that tent where he and his father will have a moment of up-close-and-personal contact. Perhaps that personal contact will actually be *too* close for comfort.

Jacob needs to come to a place where he *stops giving away his power to become who he truly is.* As long as he holds on to the false image of what he is expected to be, what he thinks he should be, he can never let go and become who he is truly meant to be.

In order for Jacob to stay emotionally balanced in the midst of this ruse, he has to creatively use a part of his own ingenuity to survive. This creative expression, deceptive as it will be, at least is a part of him and not the mask he is wearing. At least it is closer to who he really is than who he pretends to be.

You have to ask yourself a question. What kind of confidence does Jacob have in his father? If you answered that question the way I suspect you did (meaning he has none whatsoever), then answer this one: where does Jacob derive his confidence now that his mother is not there in the tent with him? He has to derive it from the only place he knows: his own shrewdness and determination to survive. This is a guy who hasn't yet had a radical encounter with the power of a God who both loves and transforms. All he knows is that the God of his father and mother has entrusted him with a legacy, and though he has never met this God, he trusts his mother enough to know there must be some truth to all of it. Yet since he has no experience with God's power, and has great mistrust for his father's power, the only power left for him to use is his own.

Jacob continues to survive as best he can by masking his true identity behind the dead skins of a substitute. This is Halloween in the tent of Isaac. How much learning had to take place in Jacob before this moment occurred? How much unlearning will it take for him to become who he really is and is meant to be? How long before he becomes fully human and authentic? In the story *The Velveteen Rabbit*, it took a long time for the rabbit to become "real" to the little boy that received him as a Christmas gift. The process of becoming real was quite painful for the rabbit, yet the more it was neglected, abandoned, and bruised, the more real the rabbit became to the little boy.

THE MASQUERADE

It is the struggles, the pains, the disappointments, and the processes that we go through that make us come to a place of being authentic and touchable to others. Jacob has a long journey to go on that begins when he comes of age, steps into that tent, and answers the question, *who are you?*

He says to his dad, "I'm Esau." In other words, "I'm my older brother for today, and I need you to hurry up and do what you are supposed to do now, because I can only play this game so long before you find out who I really am!" Jacob tells his dad to please hurry up: "Arise, sit and eat of my game, that your soul may bless me"(Genesis 27:19). Time is a precious commodity when you have to pretend to be someone you are not.

Isaac isn't about to be rushed by all this. After all, this is a sacred moment, a rite of passage. Jacob, on the other hand, has been grabbing at his brother's heels so long he can even feel when they are fast approaching. He knows if he is to have a future, it will have to be given to him quickly.

Time is a precious commodity when you have to pretend to be someone you are not.

Isaac is surprised by how quickly "Esau" has caught and prepared the prize. He has a simple question for his son: "How is it that you have found it so quickly?" Even Isaac knows that, as good a hunter as his firstborn son is, nobody is *that* good! When we try being someone else, unless we really think about the other person's beliefs and behaviors, we may put words in his mouth that he would never say. Listen to Jacob's response: "Because the LORD your God brought it to me" (v. 20).

Let's look at this closely. First of all, Esau has no interest whatsoever in the things of God. He despised the birthright and saw no value whatsoever in things unseen. Esau never would have given his father a "spiritual" answer. Esau, if he did catch something that quickly, would have bragged on his own ability. It isn't in Esau's nature to give a thought to attributing his success to a power greater than himself. For Esau, the world is all about him. So, careful observation of his behaviors and beliefs would place this statement totally out of character for Esau.

Jacob wasn't thinking on his feet here at all. However, he was revealing a part of him that still wanted to figure out a way to get his dad's approval. Jacob *did* at least have a heart for the things of God. Secondly, Jacob thought he knew what his father wanted to hear, because he knew that in spite of his dad's rejection of the word of God regarding who got the birthright, Isaac did fear God.

Jacob is wearing a mask of false spirituality here in an effort to impress his dad. This story is repeated day in and day out among the "faithful" in every city, state, and country on the planet. It is a comforting thought to know that God not only puts up with all the facades we wear, but He also uses it to bring us to a moment of truth when we are really ready to unmask, let go, and become who we truly are.

Isaac is still not convinced he is being given the truth. He says to his son, "Please come near, that I may feel you, my son, whether you are really my son Esau or not" (Genesis 27:21). Isaac cannot see with his eyes anymore, so he will rely on his sense of touch. This is too close for Jacob's comfort. You can just see the sweat beading up on his brow. He has to get close enough to his father so that he is in a place of intimacy.

Jacob has a challenge: He has never formed a deeply intimate relationship with his father. The steps between them are getting smaller, and the closer he gets, the more unnerving the experience. Isaac senses the nearness of his son and reaches out and grabs his arms and doesn't let go. Then he rubs his hand over Jacob's chest. You have to give Rebekah credit; she did anticipate all of this would happen. She knew Isaac a whole lot better than the rest of the family.

Isaac feels the skins of the goat, and they pass for the hair of Esau. He doesn't quite say he is convinced, though. Isaac's sense of touch tells him that what he feels has to be the hands of Esau. This is strange indeed. The man knows it isn't Esau's voice, yet he doesn't know the difference between goat skin and Esau's skin. It makes you wonder how intimate Isaac really was even with Esau. If Isaac could be fooled by the skins of a goat and bless Jacob instead, he probably didn't have as close a relationship with Esau as he seems to convey. Again, it would seem as if Esau simply existed to serve Isaac's appetite, and that is as far as the relationship really went. Isaac only "knew" Esau to the extent that he wanted what Esau could do for him. Did he ever really know Esau for himself? Did Esau ever really feel that much more connected to his dad than his brother did? Time will reveal that, in fact, that was not the case at all. Isaac asks one more time: "Are you really Esau? " Jacob plays out the role to the hilt: "I am."

Isaac, in his blindness, yields to the masquerade and blesses the younger son because the meal satisfied his appetite. With a full stomach, Isaac now wants his son to kiss him. Un-condional love freely gives without any personal appetite being satisfied first. Conditional love is love with a hook attached. It says, "I will give you what you want if you first give me what I want." Isaac's love is clearly conditional here. His belly is satisfied, and instead of now at least kissing his son first, he asks his son to kiss him. This has to be a tough moment. Jacob, who more than anything else needs to have an intimate relationship with his father, is now forced to play out an uncomfortable role and act as if he really wants to kiss his father. This is a mere formality, more like a family custom than a real expression of pure love. Jacob may have longed for that all his life. However, in actual fact, it is just a surface act with no real exchange of deep admiration and bonding taking place. Not only that, but Jacob has to initiate something that will be done in the name of one who is definitely *not* him.

Remember, you cannot become who you are until you acknowledge who you are not. Jacob is playing out the role of who he is not, and naturally it is leaving some lasting impressions on his heart, his mind, and even on his lips. Jacob got as close as he could get, and again, Rebekah had thought through this moment: the smell of Esau was all over Esau's garments, which Jacob was wearing. If Isaac wasn't convinced by the hands or the meal, the smell of the garments so masked the presence of Jacob that Isaac began to release the blessing of the birthright. It was now flowing out of his lips unhindered. The first part of the blessing had to do with the field and with the dew of heaven. Get this: the last place Jacob wanted to be was in the field and under the dew of heaven. Jacob liked being indoors. This was not a blessing he was interested in.

The last place Jacob wanted to be was in the field and under the dew of heaven. Jacob liked being indoors. This was not a blessing he was interested in.

Now that the trick-or-treat charade is playing out its full drama, Jacob is going to get everything that belongs to the first-born, including the territory that is required to be conquered if the blessing is to be appropriated. The smell of the field is not a smell that inspires Jacob. Jacob likes the smell of the tent, of handmade blankets made from hides that he neither skinned or tanned. Jacob likes tending the garden, not conquering the land. What is he going to do with a blessing that doesn't fit who he believes he is?

When you choose to play out the game of life and are willing to really find out who you are and who you are not, you also have to take what is given to you as a gift and receive it as an opportunity, albeit a dangerous one.

Jacob is promised the field, the dew of heaven, the fatness of the earth, the abundance of the harvest, the grain, the new wine, the command of all sorts of people, nations bowing down to him, the honor to be master over his brothers, the realization that his mother's sons will bow down to him (which, in that society included grandchildren, great-grandchildren, and so on), a curse on anyone who tried to curse him, and a blessing on all who blessed him (see Genesis 27:28–29).

This was the moment Jacob was waiting for. He got the satisfaction of knowing that what his brother thought he would get, Jacob got in his place. He probably figured that he got what he wanted . . . or did he get more than he bargained for? Did he feel good about himself? Did he really embrace what he was given? Was he aware that he had just come of age, and now things would unfold that were beyond his ability to control? Probably not. But it was too late to turn back. He left the tent thinking the conflict and the discomfort were over. It had just begun.

CHAPTER 8 | WHEN YOU CAN'T LET GO OF RUNNING FOR YOUR LIFE

So Esau hated Jacob because of the blessing with which his father blessed him; and Esau said in his heart, "The days of mourning for my father are at hand; then I will kill my brother Jacob."—Genesis 27:41

Thankfully for Jacob, it would be eighty years before his dad would pass on. He didn't know that then, but at least it would afford him some time to sort out his dilemma. Isaac and Rebekah are now faced with all sorts of challenges. Isaac's older son is mad at him for what has happened, so Esau decides to "get even" by marrying outside of their traditions.

Rebekah, on the other hand, doesn't trust Esau and knows that at any moment he could forget about his willingness to wait until his father dies to kill his brother. She figures out a way to get Isaac to send Jacob on a long journey, out into unfamiliar territory, through dangerous mountainous terrain (talk about Jacob's out-of-comfort zone), and back to the land of her family where he could find a wife who would be part of the legacy that the God of Abraham had laid out for them.

Jacob had to run for his life. He had no choice. A chapter of stability was over, and he could not go back. With all the bickering and backbiting, competition and comparison, at least it was what he was used to. Who likes endings anyway? It is easier to live dreaming about a future than actually waking up and heading there.

There is an appointed time and season for every purpose under heaven. Solomon said there was a time for birthing as well as a time for dying, a time for killing and a time for healing, a time for tearing down and a time for building up, and of all things, a time for putting down roots and a time for being uprooted. (See Ecclesiastes 3:1–8.) Well, this was one of those seasons of being uprooted.

> Who likes endings anyway? It is easier to live dreaming about a future than actually waking up and heading there.

It would be great if life just kept moving along smoothly without any major upsets. Some people wish that life would be as simple as it was for Olive Oyl, Popeye's girlfriend. Even when she was sleepwalking (an apt metaphor for not living a conscious and in-touch life), Popeye would attempt to rescue her from falling out of windows and off of high buildings under construction. She was never disturbed from her sleeping through life—everybody else did the worrying for her.

Life ain't like that. You have to be willing to experience what you have never known before. The best journey Jacob can take at this point is outside of his comfort zone into dangerous territory on his way to his uncle Laban's household. If ever Jacob felt boxed in, he won't anymore. He also has to choose an unfamiliar path that will take him a bit longer because his brother knows the wilderness quite well. Jacob is running for his life with one eye on the horizon and one eye looking back over his shoulder.

There is no doubt in my mind that fear is pumping the blood through his veins faster than normal and is causing him to pick up his pace. When the sun is about to set, he happens to stumble on "a certain place" where he will spend the night totally exhausted with a hard rock under his head for a pillow (Genesis 28:11).

Onkelos's translation of Rashi's commentary had an interesting insight on this experience in the life of Jacob. Rashi, the ancient rabbi, claims that the "certain place" was a rather specific place in the history of the journey of Abraham. We will consider that a bit more later on.

Here are some cold facts about Jacob's process of letting go. Perhaps they will assist you on your journey as well:

1. Jacob is pressed to leave, not because of a desire to follow after the destiny of God, but by Rebekah's urging out of fear of Esau's power to destroy Jacob's

future. How often have you run into your future not out of a real desire to pursue your destiny, but more out of a need to escape your past?

2. Secondly, there is a promise that a reward of a satis-fying relationship awaits him. The promise that Jacob will find the girl of his dreams if he is willing to run for his life will give him a certain motivation to move forward. However, how often have you run into your future in hopes of finding a relationship that will make you feel fulfilled, only to find that unfinished business from your past relationships was waiting to meet you again in your future ones? The way you leave a former chapter can affect the way you enter a new chapter in your life.

3. There is also this promise that if Jacob goes to his mom's family God will bless him and make him fruitful. Bearing fruit is all about obtaining the out-comes you were created to obtain in life. When I speak of achieving your vital design, I am referring to honoring that divine blueprint deep within your heart that represents your utmost for God's highest in your life. As much as the first two motives for moving forward are based on self-preservation and what tickles your fancy, this one thing touches the core of becoming who you are truly meant to be.

Somewhere in the midst of all the reasons you move forward, there is at the center of your being a longing to bear the kind of fruit you were meant to bear and obtain the kind of outcomes that you were intended to accomplish.

Jacob will be tested by the first two motives in order to be set free from running for his own life. His walk will eventually slow down to the speed of life, and he will live in "real time." The third motive that gets him running will actually be the key that unlocks the door to his hidden brilliance and untapped potential. It will be the thing that heaven uses to help him finally let go of who he has been so he can become who he was born to be. What will heaven use to help *you* let go?

CHAPTER 9 | WHEN YOU CAN'T LET GO OF TRYING TO GET PAST YOUR PAST

And he came to a certain place and spent the night there,
because the sun had set.—Genesis 28:11

When, like Jacob, you find yourself having to travel the unfrequented path, you can't avoid the rough terrain. The place
through which you must move has no familiar form and is
void of the ability to support you as you have been used to
being supported. The wilderness, the driven place, is a place
of chaos. It is unstable. It is far reaching and widespread and
can't be bypassed. The road to your next chapter in life might
be a bit bumpy, to say the least. And . . . there are no short-
cuts here to becoming who you are truly meant to be.

At the same time, the wilderness can provide you opportunity to discover things about life and about yourself that can
renew your passion and purpose for the future God has in store.
You will be invited to go on the adventure of a lifetime—your
lifetime—and it will be a time to consider your past, acknowledge your present, and head toward your future.

The ability to adapt is a key to your survival. If Jacob can find the resources to outsmart his father in the tent, he is going to need all that help and more to adapt to the world "out there" in the wild place beyond his comfort zone. That place is more comfortable for his brother, yet now that he has been blessed with what is in the "field," he has to get out there and find his treasure buried somewhere. Since he is traveling an unfrequented path, he also needs the skill and the nerve to tolerate ambiguity and uncertainty.

When you are ready to become who you truly are and let go of who you thought you were, you will find yourself being invited to tolerate uncertainty. You'll have to be willing to live with some questions that beg answers. It takes some skill to live with not knowing. In his letters to a young poet, Rainer Maria Rilke said this:

> Be patient toward all that is unsolved in your heart and try to love the questions themselves like locked rooms and like books that are written in a very foreign tongue. Do not now seek the answers, which cannot be given you because you would not be able to live them. And the point is, to live everything. Live the questions now. And perhaps without knowing it you will live along some day into the answers.

When Jacob was sent off running for his life, he was being invited to live with uncertainty. Do you know why? Because he had been blessed to do so! Like it nor not, you have been blessed to live with questions in the midst of change. Your personal history, though filled with some challenges, disappointments, unfinished business, and frustrations, is still part of what shaped you to this point.

Like it nor not, you have been blessed to live with questions in the midst of change.

Jacob is about to find out that his past will continue to wind its way into his present life. What he will do with that and how he will perceive it will affect what he gets from it.

WHERE YOU ARE

The one thing you need to remember is that in spite of the stuff you have been carrying around inside, you are the recipient of a blessing that cannot be reversed. You are going to make it, and you are going to make it all the way. You just don't know it yet.

There are certain stops along the highway called "rest stops." You've seen them. They are generally picnic areas and restrooms. Somewhere between the restrooms and the picnic area there is usually a big map posted of the state you are traveling, with a large, red arrow that says, "You are here." It is important in the journey toward becoming who you are that you have time to stop and gain your bearings and discover where "here" is. If you don't know where "here" is, you won't know if you are moving toward wherever "there" is. Sometimes an extra-long car trip can cause you to lose track of exactly where you are. A rest stop helps you to reacquaint yourself with where you are and perhaps how much farther you have to go to arrive at your destination.

As a human being, there is so much that is beyond your control. You want to feel as if you have control over something. The last thing you want is to have to tolerate not knowing. Yet you must, at least for a little while. Jacob is so used to solving his own problems in a particular way because he has had a degree of familiarity with how to control what was in his own past environment. However, he isn't in his own environment anymore. He is now in an arena that is far too big for him to manage as he did at home.

How will he handle the wild world his brother was so at home in? A world of scorpions, desert snakes, spiders, mountain lions, and bears. Where will he find protection at night? Does he have what he needs to make a fire? What if Esau sneaks up on him and overtakes him while he is sleeping?

You can run only so far on adrenaline before your body just gives out. Your mind can wrestle for hours, days, or weeks trying to solve a problem, but when it has exhausted all its avenues, grabbed for another heel to cling to, and come up empty-handed, it really is time to let go. It's time to live with the questions that have brought you on the quest.

LIVING WITH THE QUESTIONS

There are deep changes that are already taking place inside Jacob that he is not fully conscious of yet. He is seeking to form a realistic sense of who he is and who he longs to be. He is a grown man, not an adolescent, when all this takes place. He isn't "twenty-something" during this time. He is older. Historians argue and speculate about just how old he really was when he obtained the birthright by masquerading as his brother. This much all the historians agree on: Jacob is well into his adult years. He is actually going through what today we might call a "midlife transition" (sounds nicer than "crisis," doesn't it?).

Jacob is in the process of forming and reforming his personal identity . . . and so are you. He is asking questions like, *Who am I?* He might even be asking, *How much is there out there that I haven't got a clue about?* Or perhaps, *How do I get from where I am to where I want to be?* Perhaps there is the question, *What if I fail?*

Human beings resist change more than any species on the planet. When you get to a place where you embrace change as gain and growth, you are becoming who you were meant to be, and are well on your way to wholeness and healing.

Part of adulthood is living with the questions. It is one of the main things you do in your transition times in adult years. You do it consciously as well as unconsciously. Jacob is wrestling with how to interpret his past. He is trying to figure out what to let go of, what to hold on to, and how to move forward. But while trying to interpret his past, he is haunted by the thought that his past (Esau) will overtake him and prevent him from getting to his future.

There is a reason that you grow into adulthood with a need to interpret your past. If you can accurately interpret your past, you can to some degree successfully organize your present and easily move into your future. It takes abrupt changes for those opportunities to be activated, because you get used to what you know and are comfortable with. There is a part of you that wants change, yet another part of you that views change as loss. Letting go can have painful consequences. Human beings resist change more than any species on the planet. When you get to a place where you embrace change as gain and growth, you are becoming who you were meant to be and are well on your way to wholeness and healing.

A LITTLE HELP FROM A FRIEND

There are some problems, though, that Jacob can't seem to get past. He is undernourished in who he truly is because he has organized his life around the image of the one whose heel he grabbed. Feeding on the wrong foods will make you unhealthy. Feeding on a false image of who you are will starve your spirit of the necessary nutrients and soul food you need to become who you are meant to be.

While Jacob carried a ton of hopes from his childhood into adolescence, by the time he should have let go of his brother's heel, he was already feeding off of his brother's image. That image was true for his brother, yet false for him. Jacob's feeding frenzy had left him undernourished in genuine self-esteem. When you are more committed to living out of a false image than you are about being real, your esteem suffers.

Jacob, like you, still carried all his childhood hopes with him into adulthood; they are just covered with lots of disappointments. Those disappointments over the years have become almost as hard as stone. In the dark he will lay his head on stone that is as hard as those disappointments. Yet things will loosen up, and deep change will take place. Rest assured!

Once you have a clear sense of where you have been, you can acknowledge where you are and line both perspectives up (past and present) to get to where you are going (future). That is the only way you can know what to let go of, what to hold on to, and how to move forward.

You and I need a little more help than what family and friends have to offer, especially today. We live in a day when few people have much connection with their pasts. Family structures have so broken down and fractured over the last two generations that continuity seems to have been lost internally as well as externally.

People are homeless not just on our streets; they are homeless in their minds. There is a radical disconnect in the current generation with what has preceded us. What we need is a vital reconnection to where we have truly come from. You can't just get by anymore with what the Beatles called "a little help from my friends." What you really need is help from the Friend that sticks closer than a brother or sister to accurately interpret your past, organize your present, and move into your future.

God will invite you in the rough and unstable territory of transition to begin to rewrite your life story according to the original script, the blueprint inside your heart that caused you to begin life reaching for the higher possibilities (perhaps reaching for the "stars"), yet left you grabbing on to someone else's heel. Change requires letting go and moving on. Jacob has lived his life dependent upon his mom to get him through, keep him motivated, protect him, and so forth. Then he finds he is being separated to walk independently. He is on his way to a new place, a "certain" place.

YOU ARE HERE

Jacob lighted upon a specific place. He "happened upon" the place of a divine appointment. At the moment of his exhaustion, when he has spent all his strength running for his life, he reaches a place that is actually waiting for his arrival. There are places in life that are awaiting your arrival and are prepared for you before you ever get there. In those places you will experience greater and greater degrees of separation between who you really are and who your parents or primary caregivers may have said you were to be.

Staying open to the possibility of experiencing something

unexpected is a healthy way to move into your future. Having childlike trust in God as your ultimate caring Parent, and knowing that there is a prepared place waiting for you, even if you don't know its name or location, will help guide your feet there.

By the time Jacob came to that "certain place" it was dark. When you come to a place where a chapter ends in your life, the sun indeed sets on that chapter. You are at the end of something, yet you are at the beginning of something else. When the light is declining, Jacob "lights" upon a certain place. He "happens" upon a place where he will get a little help from a Friend. He will find the "you are here" message that will help him get to where he is going.

> There are places in life that are awaiting your arrival and are prepared for you before you ever get there.

The word used in the text to describe that Jacob "came," or "lighted upon" a certain place is a Hebrew word that implies "to fall upon." It is as if the place just came up on Jacob as he came up on it.[1] It is also a word used to describe the concept of interceding. When someone intercedes, he is intervening between two parties in order to reconcile differences. Jacob has happened upon a place where a Friend who sticks closer than a brother is about to intervene on Jacob's behalf as he enters a night season in his life.

The rabbis tend to equate the word for *intercede* here to the fact that Jacob more than likely was praying, since it is the same word used in other places in the Torah. I'll buy that. I suppose if you are running for your life, you learn how to pray "foxhole" prayers simply to have God get you out of trouble. Jacob runs straight into the *night!*

For you, too, the past can be reconciled to the present and can help activate the future.

CHAPTER 10 | WHEN YOU CAN'T LET GO OF BELIEVING YOU ARE ALONE

And he took one of the stones of the place and put it under his head, and lay down in that place. And he had a dream . . .
—Genesis 28:11–12 NASB

Since you and I live in a world that has been conditioned by the scientific method for well over four centuries, we have lost our ability to honor direct experience with wisdom from above. We demand answers before we launch out into the unknown. We don't want the mystery of faith—as a matter of fact, we don't want the mystery of anything. We want every *t* crossed and every *i* dotted. We want guarantees for success with little or no risk involved. We want "five easy steps" to the next level in life. I regret the disappointment you experienced when you finally found out that life doesn't work that way all the time. You cannot always obtain the mastery of circumstances based on proven methods of success; however you can gain a level of mastery over yourself. That is the place where real success takes place: self-control.

If you want to become who you were truly meant to be, you have to let go of who you have been. Grabbing for external control is what has gotten you exhausted. Even God has a difficult time on occasion with attempting to pry your fingers off of your negative circumstances so He can have room to heal you from the inside out. Sometimes God will bypass your waking life and tap into your unfinished business at that time when you have no conscious control, while you are asleep.

Jacob's mind has churned up a thousand and one things while he has been running through the mountains looking for a pathway to freedom. All he has found in the corners of his mind are dead ends. Your conscious mind is only a small part of who you are. Experts tell us that nine-tenths of your being is in the realm they call the *unconscious*. The Scriptures refer to those deep places as the heart, or the spirit.

Sometimes we think we are smarter than our ancestors because we have hard data that we use to make decisions and solve problems. You turn on the Weather Channel to see what's up with the weather. Your ancestors that lived close to the land paid attention to the domesticated animals to find out what was up with the weather. You have meteorologists, they had the cows, and quite honestly, the cows have a better sense of when it is going to rain than some meteorologists! How many times has the weather person told you one thing only to have the weather be another? Cows are always on target when it comes to bad weather (Job 36:33), and so are sheep and horses, for that matter.

Science can answer some questions. For example, science can tell you what elements make up the human body. Science *cannot* tell you what makes up your soul, though. That intangible, invisible stuff of your being doesn't have any listing on the periodic table.

Your ancient ancestors trusted in things like dreams and visions. We have learned to chalk our dreams and visions up to pepperoni pizza. Isn't it great that Joseph, the husband of Mary, didn't blame his dreams about the Babe in Mary's womb on having a pepperoni pizza at midnight? (See Matthew 1:20.) Isn't it comforting to know that Abraham didn't blame his vision of a people spending 430 years as slaves in Egypt and then coming out free on too much barbecued beef from the sacrifice he offered God the night before? (See Genesis 15:12–13.)

There are "ways of knowing" with which you and I have lost contact because we have been conditioned not to value what the ancients relied on. Yet even science in the twenty-first century is beginning to prove what the ancients "knew" from other ways of knowing about the visible and the invisible world, and about things like miracles and direct experiences with things that go beyond normal, everyday experiences.

Who would have ever thought that people would be watching television programs on major networks about angelic assistance and miracles? Of course, you would expect religious channels to carry such programming, but prime-time shows on major networks? Never! Unless, people in our society have exhausted their conscious ways of knowing what we know and are crying out of a deep hunger to connect with who we are and where we hope we are going.

Maybe the tide is turning, and ancient ways of knowing wisdom are once again gaining a place of appreciation and honor in our society. Perhaps we are becoming aware of the fact that, for all our data, we are not becoming more of who we were born to be, but are actually diminishing ourselves and becoming less. And aren't you tired of being less and settling for less? Are you willing to start crying out for so much more from a deep place inside? Perhaps the answers to your future lie deep in your past, and once you get back to your ancient history, you may discover that your forefathers found answers as they allowed their spirits to be open to direct experiences with God Himself.

Now, there is a revolutionary thought, that God, the Creator of the ends of the earth, should be able to communicate with His creation and get a message across about His intentions and designs for the human race. Why don't you check out Daniel 7:22 and tell me, if your ancient history dates all the way back to the Ancient of Days?

JACOB'S LADDER

There are ways of knowing that open up to you when you have to leave the familiar territory of your comfort zone and radically trust God for the future He has in store for you. He may lead you as He did Jacob, by way of exhaustion. However when you get to a certain prepared place, when you find yourself willing to make a hard rock a pillow to sleep on, and you are truly between a rock and a hard place, unexpected things happen!

Jacob laid his head on a rock. It was a far cry from the soft quilts his mother had made for his head to sleep on in the tents of his homeland, but he was too tired to think about the discomfort. You have to be really tired to let your head rest on a rock and be able to go to sleep.

When Jacob laid his head on that rock, his conscious mind let go of the need to solve his problems. Even if Esau was out to get him, the sun had set, and his body was too weary to keep running, his eyelids were too heavy to stay open. He entered deep sleep. Somewhere in the night his unconscious mind and his active imagination found their way to a portal into the unseen real arena of heaven itself. He had a dream for sure, yet the dream was a genuine communication from a realm beyond the world he had known.

This was a direct experience with the God of his fathers. This is totally unexpected, and totally unknown in his past experience. He has "heard" about the God of his fathers; now he is about to have an encounter with that God. And some would say it was the pepperoni pizza.

I can still hear in my memory George Beverly Shea singing his rendition of "We Are Climbing Jacob's Ladder" at a Billy Graham Crusade that I attended in New York when I was six years old. At that age I didn't have a clue what Jacob's ladder was. I just heard the man sing the song, and I knew I had heard it in church once or twice before that. I didn't know who Jacob was, and I didn't know he had a ladder. I knew my uncles had ladders to climb on top of roofs to clean out chimneys. I knew Grandpa had a ladder for when he wanted to do some painting around the house. He used to lean his twelve-foot ladder against the wall of the house, and if he felt that it needed to be more secure at the bottom, he would call Grandma out from the kitchen to hold the ladder while he climbed it. What was the big deal about some guy named Jacob having a ladder?

When Jacob rested his head on that hard rock pillow, when he put his conscious wrestling to rest, when he was willing to let go long enough to relax, he had a dream. The old Hebrew word for dream means "to restore to health." Some people never rest long enough to have the kind of dreams that can restore their sense of well-being and balance in life. Your dreams will keep you alive in more ways than one.

Sleep is a natural healer. When your thoughts are anchored in anxiety, and the grip of your fingers is stuck on the outside world, you lose sleep and vitality and health. Sleep evades your grasp, and you spend the night tossing and turning. Some people are afraid to dream because their dreams become nightmares. They are afraid of things that hide in the dark. Nightmares, though, come from things people stuff down deep inside that they refuse to look at and take ownership of. Actually, nightmares can be a real gift if you understand that the reason they scare the wits out of you is that you are running away from something that you need to face in order to be free.

This dream of Jacob's wasn't a nightmare, though; it was

actually quite a pleasant and awesome dream. It was a direct experience with the greater world, the invisible world, from which the visible world derives its existence. At the same time that this is Jacob's dream, it is also your dream. You can say this ladder that belongs to Jacob also belongs to you.

Some people never rest long enough to have the kind of dreams that can restore their sense of well-being and balance in life. Your dreams will keep you alive in more ways than one.

It isn't really a ladder like the one you would buy in a hardware store. Jacob's ladder is more like a set of stone steps that ascend and descend on something that looks like a mountain or a temple. One set of steps is going up and the other is coming down.

On those steps there are angels, messengers from God, and they are going *up* to heaven from the very place where Jacob is lying down, and at the same time other angels are coming *down* from heaven to where Jacob is. It is interesting to note the order of the dream: there are angels going up from Jacob first, and others coming down second. That indicates that Jacob has help all around him that starts with him, where he is, day and night. In other words, all around him, at his level, on earth, there are invisible helpers assigned to assist him in becoming who he is meant to be. They are also there to protect him, as well as to assist him in letting go and moving on.

In addition, they are going up to heaven because they get

their orders from the One standing above the ladder. The heavenly messengers are going up to God to keep Him abreast of their work and service, and their labor of love with His child. They are also going up to get more munitions, directions, and strategies from God to assist Jacob in ever-increasing ways. So Jacob is constantly being attended, is never left alone, and is always being given support and assistance.

WISDOM FROM ABOVE

The ladder and the angels are not the main attractions, though. The main attraction is the God of his fathers, Abraham and Isaac, whom he has never personally met. God is now introducing Himself to the heel grabber. While God is speaking from above the ladder, He is nevertheless speaking directly to Jacob. There is communication between a son of man and the Creator. God always takes the initiative in terms of these intimate experiences. He is the One who is the self-revealing, self-disclosing God. The key to intimacy is self-disclosure. The God who reveals Himself to His creatures is the God of total, unconditional love and grace. He identifies Himself to Jacob as the "Existing One" who happens to also be the God of his family tree. The "Existing One" tells Jacob about Himself almost word for word what Jacob has heard from his parents and grandparents.

Jacob has had the promises made to Abraham rehearsed in his ears from the time he was born. Even Esau could quote them in his sleep. "The land on which you lie I will give to you and your descendants. Also your descendants shall be as the dust of the earth; you shall spread abroad to the west and the east, to the north and the south; and in you and in your seed all the families of the earth shall be blessed"(Genesis 28:13–14).

The key to intimacy is self-disclosure. The God who reveals Himself to His creatures is the God of total, unconditional love and grace.

Jacob is being guided back to his deep roots by God Himself. God is the guardian of this incredible promise that now belongs to the one who possesses the birthright and the blessing. While Jacob heard the blessing from his father, he is now having an immediate and personal experience with the One who offered the blessing to begin with, who not only guards it but also transmits it and transforms those who receive it.

Wisdom from above is touching a very deep place in Jacob. The bridge between the visible and the invisible world where God and Jacob meet is being built in the processes of his active imagination while he sleeps. It is a place deeper than words . . . perhaps too deep for words. It's a picture that bridges the gap and begins to heal the deep fears in Jacob's limited life. Some of the images in his dream are symbolic (like the ladder), while others are literal (God and the angels). While things in the earthly arena seem to have shut off and he has left where he came from, heaven is opening up to him and offering him an opportunity to move in a new direction.

This encounter is to mark the beginning of a brand-new season in the life of the heel grabber. If he didn't know he was on a sacred journey before, he certainly will know it now. If he was convinced he was alone before, he isn't anymore. Jacob is getting close to something awesome, something more than he had ever hoped for or counted on, something he can't even comprehend all at once. This one encounter will take him a lifetime to fully grasp.

Jacob will be invited to accept the awareness of divine grace, love, and protection in a way he has never been able to experience from family or friends. God lets Jacob know that He is *with* him. That alone is so huge, because Jacob is being told he is not *alone*. Another is with him.

Not only that, he is promised that he will be kept, protected, and overshadowed for the entire journey he is about to take away from home, and the journey he will eventually take when he returns home. In other words, in his going out and in his return, God has Jacob covered. God doesn't just have his front line taken care of—God's got his back. What does that mean? Esau can't touch him, so he can *rest assured*. His past, present, and future are all going to be guarded and taken care of, and he is going to succeed. God is on his side. He will never be forsaken. This is total, unconditional commitment and acceptance. This is nothing but amazing grace. Jacob has never had this in his life. As a matter of fact, you'll see he doesn't even know how to respond to it or deal with it. This is all too good to be true. If it is too good to be true, though, it has to be God!

CHAPTER 11 | When you can't let go of Living an Unconscious Life

"If God will be with me and will keep me on this journey that I take, and will give me food to eat and garments to wear, and I return to my father's house for safety . . ."
–Genesis 28:20–21 NASB

When Jacob wakes up from the dream, a number of things begin to unfold in him. The story reminds me in some ways of the awakening of Ebenezer Scrooge after a night of being visited by the three spirits of Christmas. Scrooge is beside himself and is a transformed man.

Jacob's statement when he awakens is profound and often missed because of the way it is translated. He says, "Surely the LORD is in this place, and I did not know it" (Genesis 28:16). He came to a realization that he and God occupy the same territory, and yet he has been too self-absorbed to be present to God and to the moment. Jacob's awareness has undergone a fundamental shift, and a willingness to come to a place of dependence and trust in a power greater than himself is beginning to emerge.

The realms of God and the sons of men overlap all the time, and not knowing that leaves room for us to think we have the ability to put something over on God, others, or even ourselves. There is One who is ever watching and interacting, reaching out in grace and love, wooing and drawing, in an effort to bring humanity a wake-up call.

Jacob is basically admitting in his statement that he has not been present to God, present to the moment, or ultimately present to reality and to life itself. The only thing Jacob has ever been present to is himself, and now all of that is changing. He wakes up with the beginning of an awareness that he has been running from himself and probably even from God.

Until you admit that you do not know, you can never know. God has softened the tough places in the mind of Jacob. The rock-hard pillow has served to loosen up the heel grabber enough to change his awareness and outlook.

At the same time, part of that awareness is uncomfortable for Jacob. This is the guy that isn't used to intimate experiences. He and his father were never that close. For the first time, God is making Himself known to Jacob, and in such a way that Jacob is coming face to face with the fact that he is loved no matter what. This isn't about his performance or his behavior; it is simply about God's choice to love Jacob and reveal Himself to him.

Jacob isn't used to this kind of love. It will take a while getting used to. Jacob is more comfortable with love that has hooks and strings attached. This kind of love is all about what God can do for Jacob. This is about a love that has no needs that Jacob can meet. This is about a love that has no hidden agenda that demands that appetite and belly be satisfied before a blessing is dispensed. This is simply about a God who says "I'm gonna love you come rain or come shine!" Coming from a family that was deeply polarized, this was so foreign to Jacob.

Love and grace can be quite unnerving even if your heart deeply cries out for it on an ongoing basis. It isn't easy to let someone love you that much. Love with no strings attached is unusual for most. The idea that you can be totally and unconditionally accepted exposes the parts of you that really don't believe that God is that good. If God is God, then He can't be all that good! Or can He?

How do you respond to a goodness that is ready to take place at every moment of your life regardless of what you have done, where you have been, what you are doing, and where you are going? You respond as Jacob did, with unworthy suspicions about that goodness.

GETTING GROUNDED

Jacob lived within perceived boundaries of who he was. What could Jacob become if he let go of his tight hold on those boundaries? God saw something in Jacob that Jacob didn't see in himself. The intent of God here was to initiate and bring about lasting change in Jacob. In order for that to happen, Jacob has to gain enduring understanding that his soul needs to be restored and renewed and that he needs to develop as a person (something he hasn't done all that well in his own household).

This encounter with God is only the beginning. Jacob has found out something new about himself: He hasn't lived a genuinely conscious life. A genuinely conscious life is a life that is present to more than oneself. It is a life that is present to God, present to the moment, and present to everything in that moment.

Jacob's new discovery about himself was that he was basically living an unconscious life. Usually it is much easier to find out something new about yourself than it is to really make appropriate use of what you find out. There is danger that accompanies an increased awareness of truth, truth about God and truth about yourself: if you fail to integrate that truth into your experience, the knowledge you gain can lead to pride, which will lead to being dishonorable to the One who gave you the truth. The One who gave it wants you to give up living alone. When you wake up to the fact that you aren't alone, you need to make changes in your lifestyle. You can't act as if you are really important, because you now have had an encounter, a direct experience with God. That won't get you very far. This isn't the time to get puffed up.

The only antidote to being puffed up is to make sure it is grounded in your life. Humility is about things being on the ground level in your life when they have come to you from the heights of Jacob's ladder. Jacob is going to have to patiently work this new truth out by acting on it and making it real in his life. That takes humility. *Humility* comes from the word *humus* which means "earth" or "ground." You can only afford to be humble when you know you are no longer alone.

So how does the "not-alone-anymore" Jacob begin to ground this new awareness? He takes the stone that he has slept on, sets it up as a memorial altar, pours oil on the top of it, and names it "the house of God," and "the gate of heaven" (Genesis 28:17). In performing this act, Jacob is bringing a heavenly insight down out of the realm of the mysterious and into the realm of the extremely practical. The stone commemorated the revelation he received, and the oil served as a memorial of the mercy that was shown him, knowing that, though he wasn't exactly the person he was supposed to be, he was still given such a gracious gift from God.

WHO YOU REALLY ARE

Jacob couldn't have really respected himself given his behaviors. Behaviors are the result of beliefs. You have to believe some unhealthy things to behave in some unhealthy ways. You cannot possibly *feel* all that respectful about yourself when you have chosen to play out a masquerade. When you act out the role of being who you are *not* for so long, you live an imitation of a life, which is a really lonely life, and not your true-to-God life.

Jacob makes the most of this moment, this wake-up call. For the first time in his life, he is becoming fully conscious and fully alive. He will have to grow and develop from this moment on; however, this experience will become an anchor that holds him steady in the storms that lie ahead. He and the Lord are in the same place, he is not alone anymore. This newfound awareness will forever alter the direction of his spirit and, as a result, the direction of his life.

By setting the stone as an altar, he is anchoring this powerful moment. He is also creating a memorial to the experience that will serve him all the days of his life (for he will come to visit it again) and will function as a landmark learning lesson for many generations to come.

You can expect the heavens to open up to you as you learn how to let go of who you have been and become who you are, because of amazing grace. When those moments of grace occur in your life, take the time and care to learn humility, grounding those moments of awareness that come by grace in order to grow as you go. Keeping it real is what this journey is all about.

What you ground in your total life experience, you own in your journey and your story. Once that new awareness is grounded in your life story, it becomes part of your personal history. Once it is part of your personal history, it becomes a powerful force of motivation to propel you into greater levels of your destiny. You can do all that because you aren't alone!

Chapter 12 | When You Can't Let Go of Unworthy Suspicions About God's Goodness

". . . then the Lord will be my God."
—Genesis 28:21, emphasis mine

Take a peek at what lies between the *if* and the *then* of Jacob's statement. God has just made an unqualified and total unconditional commitment to be with Jacob: to love him no matter what comes, to protect him, to bless him, to increase him, to bless his descendants, and the list goes on and on. Yet Jacob still puts conditions on whether or not he will reciprocate.

What is that all about? How can you ground this incredible experience of having God with you and for you one moment, and the next moment challenge that goodness and place conditions on your response to it? To say the least, this guy is a piece of work. However, don't be too tough on him—you are the same way. This is all about your letting go because it is *safe* to be who you are.

You have to ask yourself a question: If you have lived your

whole life compelled to be what everyone else has said you should, when has it ever been safe to be who *you* are? When have you ever had the time for genuine nurturing of your developing identity? There is a world of difference between selfishness and what I call "self-fullness." To be self-full, in my estimation, requires a healthy sense of respect for who God has made you to be, along with an awareness that you can't give to others what you do not have yourself.

This idea that you exist to meet everyone else's needs is not a God idea.

You can't be unconditional in your acceptance of others when you are not that way in terms of accepting yourself. You cannot offer grace to others when you refuse to experience it for yourself. You can't affirm someone else when you are starved for affirmation yourself. Genuine nurturance of who you are is essential to living your life the way it was meant to be lived. This idea that you exist to meet everyone else's needs is not a God idea. Even Jesus didn't meet everybody's needs while He walked as a totally grounded human being, and He was the Messiah!

Jesus took plenty of time for genuine self-care and renewal. He knew that if He were to accomplish His purpose, He needed time alone, time to grow, time to replenish, time to be loved, time to be quiet, and time to simply honor and enjoy being who He was. How often do you do that? I mean *really* do that? If you don't, you just might be a person who has unworthy suspicions, like Jacob, about the goodness of God.

There is a tone of distrust and despair in Jacob's statement of "if" and "then." The word for "if" is a conditional participle in the Hebrew. Notice I said, "conditional." Even the grammar indicates that there are conditions on this word. Have you ever played the "if" game? It goes something like this: "If you'll do this, then I will promise to do that!" I have played that game in life more than once, and I have known lots of people who have done the same, even after they have experienced God's goodness.

The gift of suspicion is well dispensed in the human race. Regardless of how far back it goes in your family tree or someone else's, it is important to know that it is there whether we like it or not. It can serve to protect you when necessary; however it can also serve to shortchange you when you are dealing with Imminent Goodness Himself. God isn't good once in a while. God is good *all the time.*

UNCONDITIONAL LOVE

Why does Jacob have such a difficult time with this display of total, unconditional acceptance and commitment? He isn't used to it. In his own life experience, he has never received something for nothing. Everything he has been given up to this point has had conditions attached to it.

It isn't that he is not grateful; it's that he doesn't know how to respond to an unconditional commitment from an unconditionally accepting God. This is an aspect of intimacy he was surely not used to. Perfect love may indeed cast out fear (1 John 4:18), but first it stirs it up and exposes it before it can cast it out!

Remember the Beatles tune "All You Need Is Love"? The end of the song continues to reiterate, "love is all you need . . . love is all you need . . . love is all you need . . ." Well, if love is all you need, why do you put so many roadblocks up to getting that need met? Why are there unworthy suspicions lurking in your heart and mind when it comes to God's good intentions? If God is good all the time, why do we suspect He will do something "not-so-good" if we mess up? It has nothing to do with God, really. It has everything to do with the fact that we are part of a people that has learned well how to play the "if/then" game for millennia. We insist on confidentiality agreements because people lie. We require collateral on loan agreements because people renege on their financial commitments.

When you live in a mistrusting world long enough, you learn how to hold everybody suspect, even members of your own family, and sometimes *especially* members of your own family. Years ago, the Mills Brothers sang a tune that is still as popular as ever—it puts a smile on your face even though it tells a truth that knows that behind that smile is pain. The song is "You Always Hurt the One You Love."

We have suspicions about unconditional love because all we have known in our human experience is love based on conditions. People make and break promises, and love ends up hurting. Hurting leads to withdrawal and mistrust, alienation and isolation. Oh, sometimes you don't physically withdraw; you simply emotionally withdraw and decide you will let the other person play his or her cards out before you commit, because you've been "hurt before."

Hurt is such an illusion. Ever been around someone who has a need to tell you he's been hurt before? He sounds so much like a victim that somewhere inside, if you are growing in real true-to-God personhood, you know the real issue is that the person is just angry and is masking it as hurt. Many people have been victimized in life, this is true. However, playing the role of the victim is as manipulative as anything Jacob ever did.

If love is the answer, why is it held in such suspicion in the heart? How many thieves have been lurking in the temple of your heart, hiding behind the veil of your dreams, waiting for the right moment to come out of the dark and sabotage your success without your even realizing it is happening until it is too late?

RECONCILIATION

Unless you take time to become "self-full" and to be nurtured by unconditional love in the presence of the unconditional Lover, you will continue to play the "if/then" game. I'm not saying that love cannot bring hurt. Mother Teresa was being interviewed once by a reporter who didn't understand how she could continue to help the poor in the streets of Calcutta, knowing how many people took advantage of and mistreated her and her sisters. The reporter wanted to know how she could love without being hurt. Her response was brilliant. She said, "I have found the paradox that if I love until it hurts, then there is no hurt, only more love."

Ask any parent of a teenager if he or she has had to learn how to love until it hurts, and that parent will tell you what that is all about. Creating space that allows room for growth and change is what unconditional love is all about. There has never been a safe "space" for Jacob to develop, grow, and change. He has never had space to be self-full, so he has lived in a place where he has been self*ish*. Jacob is not sure what to do with this newfound relationship with the God of his fathers. God is getting closer than anyone else, and for Jacob, that is too close for comfort. Love is a scary thing to him. He is so used to living a separate life that he doesn't have a clue about how to be connected to God, to others, or to himself.

Ask any parent of a teenager if he or she has had to learn how to love until it hurts, and that parent will tell you what that is all about.

God, on the other hand, is modeling the kind of love that will heal Jacob and relieve him of all his unworthy suspicions about God's goodness and grace. In so doing, God is going to give Jacob room to grow and space to explore this new world. The wisdom of God is such that He knows us better than we know ourselves. God will bridge the gap of extreme separation that exists within Jacob. Over the course of time, there will be no separation between Jacob and God, Jacob and his family, and Jacob and himself.

I will say it again: you cannot give what you do not have. You cannot be reconciled to others until you are reconciled to yourself. You cannot be reconciled to yourself until you are reconciled to the unconditional love of God, who reconciles you to Himself whether you believe you are ready to be reconciled or not.

Yes, there are unworthy suspicions in Jacob's heart and mind regarding God's intentions for him. Give him some time; he just had a wake-up call to the fact that he is no longer alone. It takes time to break all the patterns of living alone, separate, and disconnected. You might even need to be patient with yourself and learn how to take time with God to be self-full.

God, who is love, creates space for Jacob and for you to become who you truly are. God is the caring Parent who knows that it will cost Him everything to love you. He will even lay down His life on your behalf to convince you of His total unconditional love. Then He will create space for you to take ownership over the robbers in your own temple until you are ready for them be cast out and your temple to be cleaned up. He'll eventually win out, and your inner temple will become a real place of intimacy that will cause others to want what you have—because they will know that you are really blessed to be who you are. Jacob did have a wake-up call at this place in his life. He will be in the process of waking up for a little while longer—it takes time. He'll wake up, and so will you.

Jacob is on his way to a safe place where there is plenty of space for him to grow, but there are still issues that have to be seen for what they are and healed from the inside out. Whenever you fail to recognize the unworthy suspicions about God's goodness and intents, it is a sure sign that there are a few stops up the road where you will be given the opportunity to see just how much those blind spots prevent you from becoming all that you were meant to be.

WHEAT AND WEEDS

God will love you enough to give you space to explore, and He will accept you exactly as you are. He loves you too much to allow you to stay in a limited place for too long. Up the road, Jacob will meet one of his relatives, Uncle Laban, who will be the spitting image of everything Jacob could become if he doesn't let God heal him completely. Sometimes the unworthy suspicions you carry about the goodness of God don't seem so bad or so unreasonable until you see them fully grown and in full bloom.

Seeds look so different from the plants and trees they grow to become. You can't tell what an oak tree will look like by observing the acorn. It looks nothing like the full-grown tree. If Jacob wonders at all about what playing charades will lead to, he will find out in short order. When you allow weeds to grow in the garden of your life, you don't realize they are there until harvest time.

Wheat and weeds look similar until they ripen to maturity. If you pull up the weeds too soon, you might also damage the stalks that will carry the golden grain of your harvest. Jacob has some weeds growing in his garden of wheat. The "weeds" in Jacob's garden will take form as his Uncle Laban. Jacob is about to be given the incredible gift of seeing what possible future is in store for him if he doesn't let go of his unworthy suspicions about the goodness of God and His loving plan for Jacob.

CHAPTER 13 | WHEN YOU CAN'T LET GO OF BEING BLINDED BY LOVE

Now Jacob loved Rachel, so he said, "I will serve you seven years for your younger daughter Rachel."
—Genesis 29:18 NASB

The whole concept of having a blind spot in your life is simply this: there is a part of you that you can't see unless someone else points it out to you. Jacob has no idea that Love is leading him straight into a place where he will come to grips with his blind spot. The heel grabber has kept all sorts of people and things in his clutches up to this point. Now he is about to grab the heel of his Uncle Laban (and vice versa), yet in grabbing Uncle Laban's heel, he will be grabbing hold of his own blind spot.

When you are grabbed by God, He will lead you into circumstances that will reveal you to yourself. Circumstances are not the things in life that make or break you. They are what God uses to reveal *you* to *yourself.* Sometimes those revelations make you say, "Ouch." It's all good, though, because God is all good!

When Jacob was born, his mom told him he was given the promise of being the heir to the birthright. His personality was formed partly around the label "heel grabber" and partly around the sense that he was the heir of the birthright. He was given both a label and a promise—and they seemed to contradict each other, for sure.

Jacob's life from the beginning is shaped by those two things that he has been given, and the conflict is part of the creative tension that God will use to make him everything he is meant to be.

CHOOSING YOUR TEACHER

Jacob grew up preferring to live indoors and cook stew. Even though he will eventually have to tend flocks, hunt game, live in the wild, and do all the other things he has no preference for, in the early days Jacob lived the life he chose to live. That stage of life can be referred to as "I am what I *will* myself to be."

Then there came that uncomfortable moment of truth when, having obtained the birthright from his brother, he had to play that role to the hilt, goatskins and all. At that point, Jacob was in the stage called "I am what I *imagine* myself to be." The only problem is that he now imagines himself to be someone totally different from who he really is.

Now we are coming to the next stage. When the human

meets the divine, and the heel grabber meets the Lover of his soul, he embarks on the stage of "I am what I *learn*." When you are ready to learn, you are ready to grow. The old adage fits well here: "When the student is ready, the teacher appears."

If you recall, you didn't have the opportunity in school to pick your teachers; they were picked for you. How many teachers would you have picked differently if you were asked for your input? I can think of at least one or two I would not have chosen, and in reflecting back, they probably would not have chosen me either.

> When you are ready to learn, you are ready to grow. The old adage fits well here: "When the student is ready, the teacher appears."

Mentors come in all shapes and sizes, and while we are not fully conscious of who we are and where we are going, it seems as though the mentors in our lives are "chosen" for us. They are, however, chosen because they mirror some things that we need to get a handle on in our own experience. Some of our mentors are given to us to bring out the best in us. Others are given to us to warn us of what we could become if we aren't willing to take responsibility for our lives.

Who picked Laban to be Jacob's mentor? Ultimately you could say God did, since God was directing his path. On the other hand, it was through the prodding of his mom, Laban's sister, that Laban was picked as the next teacher in Jacob's life.

Perhaps Rebekah had been gone from home so long she forgot what her brother was really like, or maybe he had become something she never would have suspected. It's possible that if she had known what he was like, she never would have pressed Isaac to send Jacob in that direction. However, as I said earlier, we all do the best we can with what we have at the time.

Rebekah may or may not have known what Laban was like after all those years. God did, though. And God could have intervened here, just as He could have intervened before Jacob went into the tent with skins on, pretending to be someone he was not. God could have prevented the whole thing from happening the way it did. But God didn't do that. This story is part of a larger plot that has to be fully played out. Now, here is the irony: while God does cause all things to ultimately work together for your good and for His glory, provided you value His future for your life, there is a part you play, albeit unconsciously.

Jacob unconsciously was drawn to Laban. Whatever you don't acknowledge *inside* yourself, you will be attracted to *outside* yourself. Remember, we are talking about a blind spot. Yes, God had His hand in choosing Laban, and so did Rebekah—yet Jacob did too. When Jacob began to run for his life, he was choosing to run in the direction of Laban. Whether he consciously knew what he was getting into or not, he was making a choice to move in a certain direction. Once he set that choice in motion, that decision would produce outcomes.

"IS IT WELL?"

Leaving the stone-pillow memorial, he heads for the hills where Uncle Laban lives and gets to the edge of Haran, the "land of the mountaineer." There he sees shepherds with their flocks, waiting by a well with a stone lid on it, and when he finds out they know Laban, he asks them about him. "Is he well?" and the answer he gets is, "He is well" (Genesis 29:6).

Jacob, who is about to meet his future wife, Rachel, at the well, has no idea what it means for Laban to be "well." He has no history with Laban except what he has heard from his mom and dad. Being "well" is all a matter of perspective. Laban's character is far from exemplary. If he is "well," then it might not be pleasant at all to find out what the opposite of "well" is in Laban's territory.

Laban will by far be the most manipulative, power-hungry, greedy, and self-satisfied man Jacob will ever meet in his life. And he will be the best teacher Jacob ever had on the road to becoming who he truly was born to be.

KNOW YOURSELF

The heir to the blessing of Abraham is about to serve Laban for twenty-one years. Laban is a shrewd man who knows more about himself than Jacob does. That is part of Jacob's blind spot. Laban probably also knows more about Jacob than Jacob knows about himself, and in the hands of this man, that can be quite dangerous.

Because Laban knows more about himself than Jacob does, Laban will be in absolute control of the conversation. His nature is far from self-disclosing. There will be no intimacy here; that would be risky. Laban cannot let Jacob know what he is really like. That will come in time, and by the time Jacob realizes Laban's true nature, it will be too late for Jacob to get out of the agreements he makes. Jacob will now grab the heel of his uncle, his new mentor. He will also *be* grabbed by the heel—and once he is caught, there will be no escape from Laban's grasp until school is out and it is time to graduate.

When you know more about yourself than someone else knows about you, you can control the conversation. Laban, a master deceiver and seducer, is adept at controlling conversations. He is everything Jacob doesn't want to be, and yet everything Jacob started out being. Seducers are keen observers, which is how they can manipulate people and circumstances to get their way.

Laban knows that Jacob is blind to what he is revealing in Laban's presence, as you will shortly see. As long as Jacob is blind, he will be subject to Laban's control, whether he likes it or not. Even after Jacob can say, "I once was blind, but now I see," it will be too late, because he will have already entered into a legal contract that will force him to be in that territory for three seven-year periods. And of all people, Jacob knows how binding legal contracts are. Once they are signed and sealed, there is no way out.

This is dangerous yet necessary territory for Jacob to live in for a season if he is to become his true-to-God self. It is the territory where he will say, "I am what I learn."

SELF-DISCLOSURE

As he first arrives in this territory, he sees that the shepherds cannot even lift a finger to water their flocks. The stone covering the well is too heavy. Water is scarce, and unless Laban's shepherds show up, nobody gets any! Talk about a control freak. And talk about how little there was to control. Jacob is not paying attention to all the signs of the territory he is in. He is blind to all of it. And then when Laban's employee shows up, it's all over. She is drop-dead gorgeous. She is a knockout if Jacob ever saw one.

When Jacob saw Rachel, it was love at first sight for sure. Jacob's love does, by the way, represent a stage in the development of faith in your life. We are told faith works by love (Galatians 5:6). Each of us has been endowed with a measure of faith. It is energized and operates as a result of love. Love at its core is either pure or perverted. Desire can either be wholesome or destructive, depending on the motives behind it. Either way, desire is the driving force behind the God-given faculty of faith.

Jacob will labor and work out of love for Rachel. Jacob is faith at work in the spirit of servanthood. What will help him to face his blind spot is that if faith labors by love in the spirit of service, every single obstacle can be overcome.

Jacob will model the spirit of exemplary service in the presence of a seducer, deceiver, and manipulator like Laban. Yet because he will serve in faith and work by love for Rachel, he will ultimately win over not only Rachel, but everything that Laban seeks to rob him of.

Rachel is so stunning that Jacob's love is stronger than ten men, and single-handedly he removes the stone lid over the all-too-scarce water supply in the well. He didn't even need any help. Don't tell me faith isn't energized by love and desire. This guy has made a five-hundred-mile journey through rugged terrain, and survived. How unlike Jacob is this? This is the guy who preferred being indoors. This is the guy who was voted least likely to succeed by his wild brother and stubborn father. But look at this: one glance at his uncle's employee, and five hundred long, weary, and thirsty miles vanish at the sight.

Love will energize your faith any day of the week. Once love has its focus on something, real love is more powerful than self-interest. Faith kicks in, the power goes on, mountains are moved, and stone lids covering empty wells are lifted out of the way.

Jacob is just starting to believe he really has stumbled on to good fortune . . . finally. But he doesn't see that his uncle Laban is an equal-opportunity deceiver. In those hills, culture and manners don't matter. Shepherding was supposed to be a man's job, not a job for women. Uncle Laban, though, didn't have any sons—all he had was daughters. Somebody has to keep shop, and Laban doesn't want to work that hard himself. He doesn't trust the hired hands, so he employs his younger daughter. Why not his firstborn daughter?

Jacob kisses Rachel, and then news gets back to Uncle Laban, who runs out to the well to meet him. Uncle Laban gives him the customary kiss and embrace; however, it is mere formality. Then Jacob spills the beans. It says in the text, "Then he related to Laban all these things" (Genesis 29:13 NASB). Something inside me tells me that "all these things" was a whole lot more than might have been safe to say to this uncle he knows so very little about.

As I said previously, self-disclosure is the key to intimacy. However, self-disclosure has to be appropriate in its context and with whom it is safe. Jacob is being as transparent as he knows how to be. The reason is simple: he *feels* safe. However, he really hasn't discovered what it means to truly *be* safe, and he hasn't discerned his own blind spot.

How much did he tell Laban? Did he tell him about his life at home with Mom, Dad, and his brother? Of course he did. Laban wanted to know *every detail* about his sister, her husband, the children, and their wealth. Don't kid yourself. Did Jacob talk at all about his family struggles and the trifling that went on in the tent with his father? I am sure he did. What about the encounter with God in the dream? Yes, I am sure of that as well, though Laban is far too materialistic to place any real value in God talk. But oh, that birthright business and wealth, now that is of vital interest to Laban. Jacob thinks that this is a safe place because this is "family."

Not only is this *not* a safe place to open up and disclose, Jacob's blind spot prevents him from seeing that Laban is actually sizing him up to see just how he can control him. And Jacob is giving him enough information to do just that. The more Jacob talks, the deeper he digs himself into a hole.

A Larger Purpose

Jacob doesn't realize that when he gets to Laban's house, there isn't really much around for the pickings. It will be Jacob's presence that blesses and increases Laban. It is to Jacob's benefit at this season not to know, but cunning Laban intends to mooch off of his wealthy sister's son for as long as possible. Laban has had to rely on treachery his whole life. Jacob doesn't know that. All he knows is that he is on a journey, he has received a wake-up call from God, and he has been promised the blessings of Abraham (who is well-known in these parts for how blessed he was). Laban knows exactly who has shown up at his front door, but Jacob hasn't got the slightest clue who Laban really is.

Laban doesn't want Jacob to grow; he wants to cut him down to a size that is manageable. But Laban's intentions are hidden from Jacob's view, because Jacob is oblivious to it all. As a matter of fact, Jacob's ruse on his blind father doesn't compare to the ruse of Laban on Jacob's blind spot. Jacob hasn't learned how to let go yet, so whatever seems a safe passage to his future, he grabs hold of. This time the heel grabber has caught something that won't be all that easy to conquer.

Can you remember when you were wondering how long it would be until you were done with school? When you are young, you can't wait to grow up and learn your own lessons. When you are older, you sometimes wish you could go back and learn some lessons over again.

Once taken in by Laban's seductive hospitality, Jacob sees how he can make a living for a few days and have a roof over his head. Uncle Laban is happy to have someone else do the hard work around the house and the property. So, according to Genesis 29:14, Jacob worked for uncle Laban for *free* for one month! This sure doesn't sound like Jacob, does it? Since when does Jacob do anything for free?

After a month, Laban feels just a twinge of guilt about taking advantage of his nephew, albeit a very little twinge. So he says, basically, "You can't work for me for free, (even though you are family, and I am your uncle). I guess I owe you something if you are going to hang out with us"(read between the lines here in verse 15 and see for yourself).

Jacob is not about to miss this opportunity. He is on a mission. One of the things he knows for sure he is supposed to do at Uncle Laban's is get himself a wife. Jacob has come to court his future wife, and he was so taken by Rachel that he only has eyes for her. Love is blind, you know.

But Laban has two daughters, and Rachel is the youngest. Leah is the older of the two. The Bible says her eyes were "weak." It means they lacked luster and sparkle. There didn't seem to be any passion in her eyes, and they were not attractive to a man.

Jacob offers Laban seven years of labor in exchange for Rachel. Listen, that is a "whole lotta love," no matter which way you look at it. Jacob was so in love with Rachel that those seven years seemed like only a few days to him! (v. 20). Jacob's got it bad for Rachel, and like the old love song says, "that ain't good." He hasn't got a clue what is waiting for him at the end of seven years.

Listen, seven years is a long time for other men not to show up to court Laban's daughters. When you live in the hills, options are few. How many Friday nights have come and gone since Leah has had a date? And after seven years, the oldest daughter of Laban isn't getting any younger. She might even die an old maid, and all because she has eyes that don't sparkle!

On the other hand, when the weekend comes, Jacob is taking his favorite girl out for a moonlight stroll, counting the days to when he can call her his wife. This is a seven-year engagement filled with all the romance you can imagine, and all the hearts and flowers you can find on the rough side of a mountain.

Laban, though, is growing concerned. His daughter Leah is getting more depressed by the minute, and she is looking less sparkly by the day. Seven years later, Laban has to come up with a plan. He will get her married off one way or the other, by hook or by crook. Well, he can't seem to hook a shepherd for her, so he will rip off his nephew in an effort to pawn off his unwanted daughter. It really is sad that Laban has so little regard for his own daughter that he would use deceit to get her a husband.

Leah cannot feel all that good about herself. This act of

treachery that her father is about to perform isn't going to make things any better. Something is up, and it isn't pleasant. Jacob approaches Laban. He has been keeping track of the days, the months, and the years. It is now seven years to the day, and he has paid in full by service for the girl that he loves. Laban has to give him Rachel in return.

Somewhere in all of this, Jacob is learning how to serve for love's sake and love's sake alone. Faith can never reach its maximum potential unless the fires of love are fueling it. If nothing else, Jacob is learning this lesson.

Laban agrees (at least on the surface), and he gathers all the men of the hills together to prepare for a feast. And then he waits until it is good and dark. It was customary in those days for the bride to have her face totally veiled. Under the cloak of darkness, Laban has double security. At the height of the feast, the bride is brought out of the tent and presented to Jacob, veiled in her beautiful garments. Then back into the tent Jacob goes with his bride, in the dark. It's amazing how blinded Jacob has become. The man is love-struck, and seven years of working for a crook hasn't changed his inability to see through his uncle's deceptive ways. Jacob is about to discover how big his blind spot is.

There was a time when he himself went into a tent disguised under the cloak of a darkened goatskin in order to obtain what was the right of the firstborn. Now there is a firstborn daughter, Leah, who is cooperating with her father's ruse. Sadly, she, too, is forced to be involved in an act of deception, knowing ahead of time she will not really get what it is she needs from Jacob, which is love for who she really is.

Doesn't this all sound too familiar? Jacob knew going into his father's tent that he could never get what he really wanted from his father by stealth or charade. Jacob masked his identity in obedience to his mother, acted like the firstborn, and failed to receive the intimacy he longed for. Leah masked her identity in obedience to her father, acted like the second born in the tent, and failed to receive the intimacy she longed for.

When daylight broke and the tent was opened, Jacob woke up and saw the woman in his arms was not the woman he loved. He was angry with his uncle, he offers nothing except rejection to Leah, and Laban makes some lame excuse for it all. In the meantime, Jacob is determined to be given the woman he loves. It is too late to undo the marriage to Leah; legally, this is now consummated. Again, his blind spot enabled Laban to get the best of him.

Now Laban has another bargaining chip. After the customary week of the honeymoon with Leah, Laban concedes that Jacob can have Rachel as well, but he demands another seven years for her. He has Jacob where he wants him, and Jacob is once again found grabbing at a heel. He doesn't really have a choice, and so he agrees to serve another seven years for Rachel.

How often in your life has action preceded contemplation? How often have you failed to count the cost and make careful observation of everything and everyone in the moment? Practicing the presence of God also involves practicing being present to the moment. If you aren't present to the moment, your blind spot will snare you every time! "Laban" will control you no matter how hard you try to get free when you allow action to precede contemplation in your life.

Here is something else: God could have stopped this from happening. But He didn't. Why not? There had to be a larger purpose in all of this, especially if God permitted it to happen. The more you read the story, the more you stop playing Monday-morning quarterback and saying how it *should* have worked out.

God is God, and He can do whatever He wants and permit whatever He wants, *whenever* He wants. God was in all of it: Rebekah's presence and plan outside the tent, Jacob's goatskinned charade, Esau's determination to kill his brother, Jacob's run for his life, his encounter at Bethel, his love-at-first-sight experience at the well, and Laban's cunning, conniving, and treacherous ways. God allowed it all, and God can be trusted through it all!

SELF-ACCEPTANCE

Leah and Rachel will fight for their husband's affection. They, too, will fall into the performance trap with themselves and each other, and Jacob. All of it will be to no avail. God is their God as well and will be teaching them their own life lessons. Rachel, the one Jacob loves, ironically will be as barren as were his grandmother and his mother, and he, too, will experience the testing of faith for this. The entire family system, embroiled in conditional love, will struggle to learn what it is to come to a place of accepting who they are, where they have come from, and where they are going.

Leah, the unloved, will be remembered by God and blessed with six children. None of this, though, will win her husband's affections. She will learn after the birth of her fourth son, whom she appropriately names Judah ("I will praise Jehovah"), that when all is said and done, no amount of her performance will ever be good enough for the heel grabber, because he can't give what he doesn't have. She'll finally give up trying to get his acceptance and simply receive God's acceptance, and only then will she begin to really live a life of praise to Him and Him alone. She'll find the freedom she is really looking for.

Rachel will eventually, after much heartache, have to learn how to trust God to open her womb. She'll blame everybody, including her husband, for her failure to produce children, until she realizes that God is bigger than all of that. She will finally give birth to Joseph, the dreamer, and that is when it will be time for Jacob to let go of Laban and head back home.

During twenty-one years in Laban's house, Jacob will not just obtain the two daughters of Laban. He will also be building the nation that will inherit the promised land, though he is not fully aware of that yet. The fruit that is borne from the lives of Leah and her maids and Rachel and her maids will become the twelve tribes. A mighty nation is coming out of Abraham's promise from God, and from the loins of the heel grabber. He is becoming far more than he knows.

He will also be tested and tried and manipulated again and again by Laban, and short-changed and ripped off so many times it becomes humorous. Yet Jacob will have with him an unseen Friend, one who sticks closer than a brother, who is making him into an incredible servant. Jacob will come out of every test and trial blessed beyond measure.

Laban will increase on every side, and yet seek to rip off Jacob. The only problem is that Jacob is in his learning season, and God is teaching him valuable lessons of faith and creative ability. God is with Jacob, God loves Jacob, and Jacob is falling in love with God. That makes all the difference. Everything Laban does to curse Jacob, God will—as He promised—turn it into a blessing. Laban cheated Jacob and changed his wages for the worse ten times (Jacob is keeping track). In hardship and labor, without complaint, Jacob will have learned to serve and trust in a Power greater than himself.

Jacob will win over all of Laban's flocks because of a dream God gives him and a strategy that will change the course of his destiny. Laban will get angry and seek revenge, but it will be too late. Laban will lose his grip on the heel grabber because the heel grabber is in partnership with the miracle-working God of wonders. (See Genesis 30:25–31:13.)

Jacob finally knows that he is blessed by God, and that Laban is blessed only because Jacob has been in his life. Laban doesn't have any power over Jacob anymore. He is really and truly free from Laban's grip, and it comes from the inside out!

Jacob made sure that not one of Laban's sheep or goats

miscarried. If something in the flock was torn by a wild beast, Jacob bore the cost himself and didn't pass it on to Laban (sounds as if he has developed a high degree of integrity in his business transactions, in spite of the way his mentor did business). He says that he was consumed by the heat of the desert in the day, and had frost on his eyelids by night on Laban's behalf and did it all without complaining. Jacob may have been blind before, but he is seeing all things clearly now (31:38–42). He is about to get his diploma.

By the time Jacob graduates and the learning season is over, Jacob will be a very rich man (v. 43), and Laban will have been stripped of everything he tried to control and manipulate. Laban may have been able to see Jacob's blind spot, yet God had one eye on Jacob and the other on Laban.

One last word here as this chapter in Jacob's life comes to a close: Jacob and Laban made a covenant at a place called Mizpah (watchtower). Laban named it that when he made the agreement with Jacob. The words Laban said to Jacob were these: "May the Lord watch between you and me when we are absent one from another" (Genesis 31:49). It sounds so profoundly spiritual, doesn't it? I grew up in a church where, every Sunday, the preacher would use this as the benediction to bless the people and dismiss them. He would raise his hands, make the sign of the cross, and in the most deeply spiritual voice he could muster, he would utter what I grew up believing was a blessing, since a benediction implies something good being said to you.

In the vernacular of the neighborhood I grew up in, "this ain't no blessin'—this is a curse!" That old seducer and treacherous liar Laban was basically saying to his son-in-law, "I don't trust you and I don't like you, and if you do anything else to mess with me, God is going to get you!"

Years later, when I finally read the text for myself and saw it in context, I decided to find a way to be cleansed from all the times that preacher cursed me while I was growing up! It is amazing how much religion gets in the way of spirituality. Sooner or later, you have to know that it is okay to let go and be who you really were meant to be, even if religious folk can't stand it.

CHAPTER 14 | WHEN YOU CAN'T LET GO OF THE ONE FEAR THAT WON'T GO AWAY

And the messengers returned to Jacob, saying, "We came to your brother Esau, and furthermore he is coming to meet you, and four hundred men are with him."
—Genesis 32:6 NASB

Someone once said, "What you don't face you cannot erase." Twenty-one years have come and gone since that infamous day in Jacob's father's tent. Over two decades have passed since Esau uttered those vengeful words that he would take his brother's life once his dad had died. Isaac is still alive, but so, it would seem, is Esau's anger. And that isn't all that is still alive. Jacob's fear of Esau is alive and well. Even though he buried it under layers of cold nights and hot days serving his uncle Laban, growing a big family, and getting really rich, the fear was still there.

No matter how much God has blessed Jacob, no matter how many things God has proven to Jacob, no matter how many things God promised him at Bethel, Jacob still was not convinced

God was big enough or loving enough to handle his older brother. Jacob was more afraid of Esau than he was of anything else in the world.

After years of living with regret, guilt, and perhaps with "if only I had handled this whole thing differently," Jacob is facing his old fears, which have returned with renewed fury. There is a battle royal raging in the heel grabber's heart. He is afraid for his life. He has conquered so much in these last years. He has learned how to serve, and he has even learned how to love the unlovely (Laban) as best he can. He has discovered how to be fair in his business dealings. He has learned how to recognize divine guidance. He has also learned the obedience of faith. He has walked through rough territory and let go of so much. Yet, he still is clinging to his deep-seated fear of his brother.

God is a God of love, perfect love, unconditional love. God may have rejected Esau for his attitude toward the birthright, yet He didn't leave Esau without some family blessing. Esau, too, has spent twenty-one years thinking about where he has been, what he has done, and how he has fared. There was a part of the blessing that his father gave him that he still hasn't experienced, either: "By your sword you shall live, and you shall serve your brother; [but] it shall come to pass, when you become restless, that you shall *break his yoke from your neck*" (Genesis 27:40, emphasis mine).

Neither brother has had any sense of peace for twenty-one years. Things are coming to a climax, and the inevitable is right around the corner. What they both need to realize is that the struggle is not with one another, it is with themselves. All the resistance they are encountering is inside their own hearts. What would it take for you to end the struggle against yourself?

When you are stuck in some deep-rooted fear, the only way out of it is *through* it. You have to face your fears. Perfect love cannot cast it out until you are ready to face it and take ownership of it and then walk it out.

You have to face your fears. Perfect love cannot cast it out until you are ready to face it and take ownership of it and then walk it out.

By now, Jacob has had many years of spiritual and faith formation. At the same time, he still refuses to give God this one area. He is, after all, the "heel grabber," and it is Esau's heel he still cannot let go of. He still has one more river to cross and one more confrontation to face before it is safe for him to be who he truly is.

FACE TO FACE

God has already told Jacob to pack his bags, kiss Laban good-bye, and head home. Jacob is ready to get back home and see his family. Meanwhile, Esau has established himself in the land of Seir, which means "hairy" or "shaggy." The Bible says that as Jacob "went on his way" toward his brother's territory, he had another direct experience with God: the "angels of God met him" (Genesis 32:1). It's become quite a thing for Jacob to have encounters with angels. When Jacob saw them, he said, "This is God's camp," and he "called the name of that place Mahanaim" (v. 2), meaning "double camp." In other words, there were two camps, or companies, of angels. Again, Jacob is being invited to see the larger world and acknowledge that there is more going on than meets the eye.

Jacob wants to respect boundaries, and he obviously knows his brother's whereabouts. He certainly knows enough about his brother's exploits to know how powerful he has become in his own right. Jacob's encounter with the angels at the place he names "double camp" (of angels) prepares him for a supreme ordeal that will end in a face-off with Esau.

Esau has multiplied his talents and reproduced himself, and has raised up a large number of trained warriors and hunters. They will later become known as the Edomites. Jacob sends messengers ahead of him to let his brother know that he is returning from Uncle Laban after all these years, and that he has been blessed with plenty of livestock and servants. By doing this he hopes that, if he can placate his brother with a gift, there won't be any fighting on the way back home. All of this strategy is fear based, not faith based.

The messengers don't get all that far, perhaps a day's journey, and they head back to Jacob, because Esau was a lot closer than Jacob realized. The word they brought Jacob was kind of like a "good news/bad news" report. It went something like,

"Guess what! Esau is on the way to meet you. By the way, four hundred of his top-trained security team are with him." That is all Jacob had to hear. His fear began to multiply. He was envisioning the worst-case scenario and hadn't even read the book about how to cope with it. His adrenaline rushed faster than it had in a long time. His blood pressure began to climb, and he was breathing quite heavily and in a labored fashion.

Jacob now decides to make a connection between what he saw in the vision of the two camps of angels and what to do with his wives, children, and servants. He divides the wives and children up into two groups: Leah's maids, servants, and children in one group, and Rachel's crowd in the other. He divides up the livestock as well, and sends both companies off in similar, yet different, directions. His hope is that if his brother goes crazy, at least some of Jacob's family will have a running start and a fighting chance.

Then Jacob has one of those moments of truth when he opens up and prays one of those genuine, transparent prayers. He calls on the God of his fathers, and then reminds God of His leading and guiding and His promise to be good to him. He also reminds God that it was He who had said it was time to head back home. All of that is fine. Then he gets as real as he can. (When you are faced with the fact that there may not be any way out, you do get ruthlessly honest with yourself.) He tells God that he isn't "all that," and, as a matter of fact, he is less than worthy of the unconditional love and grace that God has shown him. He lets God know that he knows where he came from (32:8–9).

When Dad sent him packing, the heel grabber had nothing in his hand except the staff, the tribal birthright—a dead stick with the family history etched on it and given to the firstborn son to be preserved from generation to generation. When Jacob crossed the Jordan and headed up the King's Highway through Damascus and on the way to Haran, he leaned on that dead stick for support because it was the only friend he had. In other words, all that he had to comfort him when he left was the testimony of where he had been, which for the Hebrews was etched on his staff. When you need it most, the staff of your personal history will be God's instrument of comfort when you enter life's transitions and cross over boundaries to enter into new life chapters.

Jacob reminds God of all that God put in his empty hands as a result. He went out with just his history in his hands, and he is returning with two companies of people and an incredible amount of riches. Yet there is one other thing he carries with him, and it apparently has also grown bigger through the years: his fear of his brother.

All he wants from God is for Him to protect his wives and children and deliver him from Esau. He commits himself into the care of God and finishes praying. He then prepares a sizable gift for his brother and sends it on ahead with some of his servants. He instructs them to let Esau know that what is being sent is a gift from Esau's "servant" Jacob. Wow! Jacob is sending word that he is his brother's servant. This is a major attitude adjustment. The heel grabber now acknowledges that he is

Esau's servant. American essayist Robert Greenleaf, revered as the grandfather of new paradigm thinking, was known for saying that our generation no longer needed leaders who served, it needed servants who lead. Jacob has become a servant-leader.

Jacob is not interested in lording it over his brother. He isn't interested in being one up on his brother. Working for Laban has taught him that if he can serve Laban in an honorable way, how much more can he serve a brother whom he swindled out of the birthright years ago? He wants to repay his brother for all the grief he created for him. This is not the same man that Esau knew twenty-one years earlier.

Interestingly enough, he sends the gifts over ahead of him because he hopes to *appease* Esau. The idea in the Hebrew here for the word *appease* implies "to make atonement for." Jacob really and truly wants to make up for all that he has done to harm his brother. However, what is even more revealing is why he wants to make up for it. Listen to his own words: "I will appease him with the present that goes before me, and afterward I will see his face; *perhaps he will accept me*" (Genesis 32:20, emphasis mine). Take a good hard look at the *one thing* Jacob wanted from his brother more than anything else: *acceptance*.

I had the privilege of knowing the late E. V. Hill in a small way through the years. I had the opportunity to interview him as a host on national television programs. But better, I often had the supreme honor of preaching alongside him, on a number of occasions, in conferences where we shared the drive from the hotel to the speaking engagements. I will never forget hearing him tell stories of the pain and rejection he went through in his years of service. He made a statement one night while preaching that still rings in my ears: "When I get to heaven, I just want to be understood."

I think about how often people so easily reject others and cannot accept them for who they are. They just don't understand them, or they refuse to understand them.

It wasn't just his father's acceptance Jacob craved; it was also his big brother's. Jacob wanted to be understood. Instead, every time he encountered his brother, the two of them were instantly at loggerheads. He wanted the struggle to end. He didn't realize the struggle was in himself, and he didn't realize he had already made some pretty big strides in the healthiest direction possible. The heel grabber is on his way from "heel to healed." However, there is one more moment that will seal it for sure. That moment will seem like eternity, and like every other significant moment in his life, it will take place when it is dark and he cannot really see all that well.

That night after he divides up the two companies, he sends his wives, their maids, and the children ahead of him, kisses them good-bye, and probably offers them some assurance that all will be well. He doesn't quite have the faith of his granddad here who, as he ascended the mountain range in Moriah with Isaac, told his servants to stay at the bottom and that he and the lad would both return (Genesis 22:5). Abraham had faith that God could raise dead things back to life. Jacob simply has faith that something will survive him, even if he doesn't.

Finally, Jacob crosses the ford of Jabbok. (Jabbok means "the place of emptying.") Once again, the only thing in his possession is his staff, a dead stick that has a little more history etched on it now than it did twenty-one years earlier.

The story goes on to say that Jacob was then left *alone*. There is that painful word again: *alone*. Your "Jabbok" is the place where you are left empty and alone to face yourself and end the struggle. Whatever ideas Jacob had about all the possessions he acquired were sent over the ford of Jabbok along with those possessions. Jacob gave it all up at that point. Whatever he conceived he had become, or might have become, he let it go that night there in the place the Hebrews called the place of evacuation and dissipation.

If you remember, I said earlier that you can have it all . . . you just can't have it all in the present moment. Well, you can go one step further. When you give it all up, and it no longer has you, more than likely you can have it all back, because then it no longer has the same power over you. The "stuff" no longer defines you. Who you are is more than meets the eye—it is who you are *in your essence*, not in what you have in your hand. Whether he likes it or not, Jacob has to let go of everything, even his fear of death, and the only way to overcome that fear is to experience it once and for all. It is the same for you. Your bad feelings won't go away by ignoring them or suppressing them. They will only go away when you own them, face them, and wrestle through them until they lose their grip on you.

CHAPTER 15 | YOU CAN LET GO NOW: IT'S OKAY TO BE WHO YOU ARE

Then Jacob was left alone, and a man wrestled with him until daybreak . . . Then he said, "Let me go, for the dawn is breaking."—Genesis 32:24–26 NASB

Jacob feels as if he is back where he started, yet, in fact, he is moving forward to a place he has never been before. Another chapter in his life is over. He thinks it is the end of his life; it is only the beginning. He has surrendered all of his stuff, all of his relationships, and all of his ideas about the way it should or must be, yet he doesn't give it up without one final struggle. This time he is fighting for his very life (at least that is what it feels like to him).

THE STRUGGLE WITH THE STRANGER

In the dark, all you can really see are shadows. Like his father Isaac in the tent, his vision is now limited by the dim light of the fallen moon. The best he can do is discern outlines against the backdrop of the wilderness and the brush beyond the river.

All of a sudden, out of nowhere a "man" grabs hold of Jacob and doesn't let go. There are a number of words for "man" in the Hebrew language;[1] this one is the word that implies a champion, a great man, a ruler of sorts. The seasons of a person's life are marked by both continuity and change, times of relative stability and great chaos. You cannot become a champion unless you have first been wounded. The word in the Hebrew for the "frail or mortal man"[2] or the "frail" implies the season of life you endure when you become aware of your weakness. That is much like going to war and enduring a transition period where you lose a few battles that you didn't expect to lose and perhaps even get wounded in the process.

This "champion" that is wrestling in the dark with Jacob in the waters of the Jabbok is "unknown" to Jacob. But Jacob probably believed that Esau had sneaked up on him and he was wrestling, once and for all, with his brother. Before this is over, somebody is probably going to lose his life.

In Jacob's mind, this was one champion fighter who was willing to fight to the death. Jacob couldn't see him, just as he couldn't see who Leah was under cloak of darkness—and as his father couldn't see Jacob as he fraudulently obtained the birthright.

Think of all the emotional turmoil Jacob is going through. He wants to make up for all that he did to his brother, but there is no room for chitchat here, let alone deep discussion. This champion has only one thing in mind: "Let's get it on!"

Jacob has so much adrenaline coursing through his veins that he cannot let go of fighting for his life. All night long, the pain of years of rejection and fear of further humiliation are being translated into raw, human, fighting energy. Jacob again feels like a loser, doing his best not to be thrown and undone. He is giving this champion a run for his money, and he is not to be underestimated. His pain has made him strong. If Jacob thinks this is Esau, then something in me says that, in spite of everything he prayed a few minutes earlier, that is all thrown out the window now . . . "Forget this servant stuff; my brother wants to kill me! I have no choice but to give him the thrashing of his life!" Jacob is putting back on his brother (so he thinks) all the pain his brother has left him to live with.

There are things that happen to us in relationships that can be quite painful. However, if your desire is to get even, your heart needs to be healed. Esau could not handle all that Jacob wanted him to feel of his own pain. Esau had too much of his own. Have you ever heard the expression "hurt people *hurt* people"? There is truth in it somewhere. When people touch their pain, they want you to feel the brunt of it if you are the one wrestling with them at that moment. No human being on the planet was built to take the beating for your unfinished business, even if it has to do with him. There is too much there to absorb, simply because others have enough pain of their own.

However, this champion is taking it all and then some. He is absorbing the blows and coming back for more. He is not only absorbing the blows, but he is also giving Jacob the opportunity to find out what *he* is made of. Jacob is winning in the fight of his life, and he is starting to *feel* like a winner.

No human being on the planet was built to take the beating for your unfinished business, even if it has to do with him.

Somewhere before the break of day, it dawns on Jacob that he is not wrestling with Esau. It also dawns on him that he is no longer wrestling with himself. He is wrestling with *Someone* who seems to know him better than he knows himself, and though this Champion is silent, His very Presence is communicating life to Jacob. This Champion isn't just bringing out the pain in Jacob; He is bringing out the prince!

Years ago, when I was growing up, my late grandfather told me, "Go out with people who are ahead of you in life, spend money on them, and treat them well. Invest in them so you can become like them." Pretty good wisdom from an Italian immigrant with only a sixth-grade education, wouldn't you say? He also said, "If you walk with a man who walks crooked, you are going to walk crooked." Both statements reveal wisdom about the quality of our lives and the company we keep. We become like those we associate with, whether for good or for not so good.

The dawn is breaking over the horizon in the eastern sky, and the shadows of the night are fleeing. Jacob no longer sees the outline of a man; he is face-to-face with Someone he doesn't quite know, yet Someone he feels he has met before. The Stranger makes a request: "Let Me go, for the day breaks" (Genesis 32:24).

The truth is, the last time Jacob saw this individual was while the angels were ascending and descending a ladder that connected heaven to earth and God to Jacob. According to Hebrew tradition, the angels ascend from us at the "breaking of the day" when they are all expected to appear before the throne of God for fresh strategies, insights, and support for you and me. This Stranger who is wrestling with Jacob knows exactly what time it is and has an appointment to keep up on top of that ladder. Whereas before, this Being was standing above Jacob on top of that ladder, this time that Being has come down the ladder, spent the night with Jacob on his level, met him where he was, fought with him through all his unfinished business, and helped him to empty all his fears in the waters called "the place of emptying" (Jabbok).

Jacob wouldn't let Him go. Ever wonder what Jacob was holding on to with such a viselike grip that the Champion couldn't get up that ladder? You guessed it: His heel. Someday, this Champion would come down that ladder for a longer period of time, thirty-three years to be exact. And that heel that Jacob was holding would one day be pierced with a large spike in fulfillment of an ancient promise, a promise much older than the one made to Jacob's granddad, Abraham.

That ancient promise said that the bruised heel of this Champion would crush the very authority of hell's dominion over mankind itself, and from that bruised heel, life would flow, and human beings would be able to once again walk in the freedom of the sons of God. He would indeed take all the abuse for your pain and mine. He would carry it in His walk up to the garbage heap outside the dung gate in Jerusalem. All our faults, failings, angers, frustrations, manipulations, deceits, and treacheries would one day be absorbed in the greatest wrestling match of the universe. The chief imp of hell himself would be crushed under the heel of the Champion and every Jacob on the planet would be free to finally let go of who they had been to become who they were born to be.

Knowing this future, the Stranger asks quite politely for Jacob to loosen his grip on His foot. He has to get up that ladder and give marching orders to the hosts of heaven for the affairs of the new day that is dawning, and part of those orders have to do with the heel grabber's future, which is now a sure thing.

Since he can't win at Jacob's level, He decides that the only way to do it is to pull rank. This is the Prince of Peace Himself who has all power in His hand. His little finger lit up the world and hung the moon and the stars in place. Yet when He comes down to the level of the heel grabber, He makes Jacob a winner, and He willingly loses. Talk about unconditional love and acceptance. Talk about God coming down to your level and letting you win in a battle against Him. Think about it: you have lost everywhere else, and then all of a sudden you win with God, and God enjoys losing to you!

BATTLING THE CHAMPION

My dad is in heaven now, and I miss him dearly. When I was a teenager I had my season of doing wild things. I got on a gambling kick back then and began to shoot dice. I got lucky and started winning games with my uncles and my school chums, and I accumulated quite a few hundred dollars over a short period of time. It was summertime, school was out, and I was working for my dad's business. I was out on service calls with my uncles during the day, and when the day was over we would head back to the office, park the trucks in the garage, and shoot dice in the back of the garage. My dad observed my behavior from afar and, while he was concerned, he chose to act with wisdom that I would not understand until years later. Now I wish he were here so I could just say thank you once more for the valuable lesson he taught me (one of the many I learned from my dad).

It was a Friday night, and he had come home from the office. It had been a good week in the business he owned, and he brought home a large chunk of cash. He placed it on the dining room hutch, and we sat down to have dinner. After dinner he said he had "heard" that I had beaten his brothers out of money that week in a few dice games. I told him that I had indeed won quite a bit of cash from them.

Dad was in World War II and was at one time good with dice. But he had long ago stopped gambling and had no desire to return to it. That much I knew. So what followed was quite out of character for my father.

167

He decided that night to become a gambler again (he did it for my sake, though I did not know it). But I didn't realize what he was gambling on. The roll of the dice is quite unpredictable unless you have loaded dice. I didn't have loaded dice and simply had been on a lucky streak for a series of games. That lucky streak turned into more than five hundred dollars, and for a sixteen-year-old boy in 1970, that was quite a sum.

I wasn't fully conscious of the value of a dollar at that age. I was just beginning to work and earn money; my dad had been working since he was twelve years old. He worked his way through college, and after the war, through business college. He labored hard with Grandpa, working with his hands and by the sweat of his brow.

Dad grabbed his five-hundred-plus dollars off the dining room hutch and told me to go get my "wad," as he called it. I asked him why, and he said he wanted to play dice. I gave him a hard time, but he insisted and acted as if he really did want to shoot dice. I knew enough about his days in the army to know that Dad knew how to bet on dice and had a reputation for being good at throwing them. I saw an aspect of my dad's history that night that I had never seen, and a face that I was not familiar with. I met the former gambler.

He was good, really good. However, I didn't realize at the time what he was gambling on. He was actually not gambling on winning. He was willing to gamble that I would stay on my lucky streak and beat him. Well, I started to win a few throws, and I wanted to quit. Dad, however, who was a gentleman's gentleman, insisted that since we put all the money on the table, we had to play until all the money was won. Now I was getting really uncomfortable. I didn't like that I was on a winning streak. I didn't like that Dad's pile of money was getting smaller and mine was getting larger. I did my best to throw poorly, but the dice kept coming up in my favor. Dad lost all his money that night, and even when I begged him to take it all back and then some, he refused and said that I had to be a gentleman and honor the rules of the game. He went to bed and slept like a baby, even though I know it had to hurt to lose all that extra cash.

There were many things that needed to be taken care of around the house that the money could have gone for. However, it was mine now, and he wouldn't let me give it back. I didn't sleep at all that night. I cried and I struggled. But Dad never brought anything up the next morning, or the next week, month, or year—or ever again. He woke up in a great mood and was happy to just relax and spend the weekend with me. I, on the other hand, had a difficult time being able to enjoy the weekend.

That was the last time I ever threw a pair of dice, and it has been well over thirty years now. Dad is in heaven, probably smiling over the choice he made that night to gamble on my beating him in dice—because though it looked as if he lost, he really won: his son never gambled again. Somehow, I think there was an unseen Hand guiding him in his actions that night, and that same unseen Hand was controlling the outcomes of the dice. The wise king Solomon said, "The lot is cast into the lap, but its every decision is from the LORD (Proverbs 16:33).

God gambled on Jacob beating Him that night. He played the game well. Now it was time for Jacob to let go. The new day was dawning; the work of transformation was almost done.

Jacob refused to let go, so the Champion reached out and simply struck the socket of Jacob's thigh, so that Jacob's hip was dislocated while they wrestled . . . now, that *had* to hurt. This was a move that Jacob didn't expect and wasn't prepared for. They say that all is fair in love and war. Was this love or war? I think it may have been a little of both.

But neither the request for Jacob to let go nor the dislocation of his hip makes him loosen his grip. He is still the heel grabber come the breaking of the day. However, Jacob does acknowledge something. He says, "I will not let You go unless You *bless* me" (Genesis 32:26, emphasis mine). What does Jacob know now about this Person that causes him to be so bold as to ask Him for a blessing? Somehow Jacob has figured out that this is no ordinary human being and that, for the first time in his life, he has a handle on Someone who really can bless him, speak well of him, see him for who he is, honor him, and give him a sense of dignity. He certainly isn't asking for more sheep, cows, silver, gold, or children (he already has more than enough). He wants a blessing that will touch the deep core of his being. He wants to come to a place where it really is okay for him to be who he is. He wants to let go and end the struggle against himself. The Stranger responds willingly and says (while He looks down at Jacob clutching at His heel), "What did you say your name was?" Jacob looks up the ladder at Him, sees those eyes looking at his vise grip on the man's heel, and says, "My name, you ask? Uh, . . . they call me 'heel grabber.' Can't you tell?" at which point the Stranger says, "That is what *they* called you." He was, after all, named based on his behavior fresh out of his mother's womb. "But that really isn't who you are," the Stranger continued. "Long before you ever arrived here, I had picked out the name of your destiny, and now I am going to give you the gift you've been looking for all of your life. You can let go now; your name is *the Prince Who Prevails with God and Men!*"

Jacob immediately lets go in awe, wonder, even shock. He has to take a moment to absorb what he has just heard. Not only that, now he needs to have faith and receive what it is he was just told. Faith comes by hearing, and hearing by a word from God. He isn't a heel grabber; he is a "prince" who has not only prevailed with men, but even with God. That is no small feat, but this guy has done it, and he has just been honored with a name that will be his entire legacy from generation to generation: Israel.

Now take notice, the Champion who wrestled with him is called *iysh* in the Hebrew tongue. The heel grabber now has "Iysh" in his new name. The first part of his name means he has taken on the nature of the Champion with whom he wrestled. He is the new crown prince in Abraham's line, and forever the nation that comes from his loins will bear his name. They will all now be called Israel. At last, he can let go of seeing himself as a heel grabber and honor the fact that God sees him as a powerful prince who can prevail in *any* situation. How's that for a boost in self-esteem?

Israel-formerly-Jacob asks the Champion a question. He wants to know what *His* name is. The response is simply this: "'Why is it that you ask my name?' And he blessed him there." (Genesis 32:29).

The prince has been named by the Champion. The mystery of His essence and nature is beyond comprehension and cannot be contained in all its fullness in any human. Eventually, this Champion will be given a Name which is above every name, that at that Name every knee will bow, and every tongue will confess it so.

Jacob-now-Israel realizes he has just seen God face-to-face. No more blind spots. This was the most intimate encounter he could ever have wished for, yet never in his wildest dreams would have believed it could happen to him. He names the place Peniel, "the face of God" as the sun begins to rise, and he limps over the place where he and the Champion wrestled all night. Even though he, too, is a champion, the prince will now walk as a wounded healer for the rest of his days. God will have left his mark on a hollow place in Jacob's life, and Jacob-now-Israel, heel grabber-turned-prince will remember that moment forever, because he will be left to walk with a limp from now on.

But at least he is able to finally let go, because it is now finally safe to be who he is: a prince who prevails with God and with men!

CHAPTER 16 | WHEN YOU CAN'T LET GO FOR LOVE'S SAKE

But Esau ran to meet him, and embraced him, and fell on his neck and kissed him, and they wept.—Genesis 33:4

A number of years back there was a great sci-fi thriller with Lou Gossett Jr. and Dennis Quaid, called *Enemy Mine*. Lou Gossett Jr. played a Draconian, and Quaid played an Earthling.

In this movie, the Earthling and the Draconian are fighting out in the galaxy somewhere and crash-land together on an alien world. They are the only two individuals on this barren planet, and they hate each other. They have been taught to be enemies, but now they will have to learn how to be allies just to survive. The enemies become brothers at a moment when they dared to be brothers.

As Jacob comes limping over Peniel (the face of God), he is extremely aware that he has just seen God face-to-face and is alive to tell the story (if anyone would believe him). As he comes across the broad plain with the Jabbok behind him, he can see his wives, his children, his servants—and his brother. Strange though, none of them expected to see someone partially crippled walking toward them in the light of the new day.

He is halting in his steps, and he is incapable of running from anyone anymore, including Esau, and mostly himself. He has to face the music and dance as best he can on one foot. However, he has just seen the face of God. He has seen the true image of Life itself, and everything is so different this morning. He is becoming what he has beheld.

He doesn't know what to expect from Esau, but he surely isn't afraid anymore. All he has in his heart for his former enemy is total unconditional love and acceptance. What he wanted most from his brother, he got from God, and now all he wants is to give that to Esau. He doesn't need his brother's acceptance anymore; now he is a prince who wants to give acceptance to his brother.

Somewhere in that night, God had also been working on his brother's heart. Gone was the will or the wish to kill Jacob. Esau wanted his brother to be free and enjoy the life he had been given. He has been blessed too. He has worked through his anger. Somewhere between the darkness and the light of the new day, when Jacob's heart was changed and his unfinished business was dealt with, something changed in his twin brother. Jacob wasn't the only one that let go—Esau did too . . . all in one night.

I don't know how long their embrace lasted, but I do know that every fear melted into peace when they held each other in their arms, and their hearts were cleansed by each other's tears.

174

This was a powerful moment. By the way, there were still powerful promises for the descendants of Esau (Edom), and they spoke of a new agreement where both the sons of Israel and the sons of Edom would be included in the promise of reconciliation.[1] Esau's descendants became the Gentiles, and even though God had to deal with Esau because he devalued spiritual things, in the end, God was going to love them back into the new agreement, based on the crushed heel of the Champion who wrestled with Jacob all night long.

Finally, and this is a powerful moment, Esau just wants to love on his brother, while Jacob insists on Esau's receiving his incredible gift as a token of love, acceptance, and forgiveness. Esau says that he has plenty and doesn't need what Jacob has. In other words, God really has blessed him, in spite of his anger, just as Isaac promised. God blessed Esau in the most unlikely and seemingly unblessable places in the land. The man has come into his own and has no need of anything from Jacob. Yet Jacob persists, and he indeed prevails. Here is what he says: "No, please, if now I have found favor in your sight, then take my present from my hand, *for I see your face as one sees the face of God, and you have received me favorably*" (Genesis 33:10 NASB, emphasis mine).

Isn't it amazing that after seeing the face of God, Jacob sees that same face in the face of his brother, who at one time was his enemy? How is it that he now sees God's face in his brother's? How is it possible to see goodness where you used to see fear? How is it possible to see love where you used to see indifference, even hate? How can you see favor where you once saw a curse?

After all of Jacob's encounters, he had finally become who he really was meant to be—and God liked it. The "prince," not the "heel grabber," was who Jacob really was, and this "prince" had learned, centuries before Jesus Christ Himself spoke the words, that "blessed are the pure in heart, for they shall see God." Jacob's heart had been purified, and the pure of heart see God in everything! *That's* why he could see God in the face of one who once only had murder on his mind.

Have you learned anything? Have you traded your "goatskin" for your true identity in Christ? Have you "let go and let God," and has He succeeded in making *you* pure in heart? Have you begun to see God—in everything? Even the pain, disappointment, and perhaps even heel grabbing in *your* past? If so, then . . .

You really can let go now . . . it's okay to be who you are!

NOTES

CHAPTER 3

1. 535 תָּם [*tam* /tawm/] adj. 13 occurrences; AV translates as "perfect" nine times, "undefiled" twice, "plain" once, and "upright" once. **1** perfect, complete. **1A** complete, perfect. *1A1* one who lacks nothing in physical strength, beauty, etc. **1B** sound, wholesome. *1B1* an ordinary, quiet sort of person. **1C** complete, morally innocent, having integrity. *1C1* one who is morally and ethically pure. From *Theological Wordbook of the Old Testament* by R. Laird Harris, Gleason L. Archer, and Bruce K. Waltke (Moody, 2003).

CHAPTER 9

1. [*paga*` /paw·**gah**/] v. A primitive root; 46 occurrences; AV translates as "fall" 12 times, "meet" 11 times, "reach" seven times, "intercession" four times, "intreat" twice, "entreat" once, and translated miscellaneously nine times. **1** to encounter, meet, reach, entreat, make intercession. **1A** (Qal). *1A1* to meet, light upon, join. *1A2* to meet (of kindness). *1A3* to encounter,

fall upon (of hostility). *1A4* to encounter, entreat (of request). *1A5* to strike, touch (of boundary). 1B (Hiphil). *1B1* to cause to light upon. *1B2* to cause to entreat. *1B3* to make entreaty, interpose. *1B4* to make attack. *1B5* to reach the mark. From *Theological Wordbook*.

CHAPTER 15

1. 376 אִישׁ [*'iysh* /eesh/] champion; great man. *Ibid.*

2. 582 אֱנוֹשׁ *'enowsh* /en·oshe/ man, mortal man, from the root אָנַשׁ אנושׁ *'anash* /aw·nash/ that means to be weak, sick, frail. *Ibid.*

CHAPTER 16

1. See Amos 9:11–12, the "remnant of Edom." Esau's seed represents the coming in of the Gentiles into the New Covenant based on the finished work of Jesus Christ. There will be ONE new man, and the enmity will be abolished because of the sufferings of the Messiah.

ABOUT THE AUTHOR

Mark J. Chironna is a physician of the soul. He is the founding and senior pastor of Master's Touch International Church in Orlando, Florida. He is a trained and certified life coach. He is also the Bishop of Legacy Alliance, a growing network of leaders and workers in the church who embrace the idea of making the gospel relevant to this generation.

Acknowledgments

I want to thank my wife, my life partner Ruth, for having the grace to give me up for the many hours and hours of laboring again and again over the manuscript of the book you now hold in your hand. Her never-ending patience and understanding is an ongoing inspiration to me. I also want to thank my boys, Matthew and Daniel, for teaching me how to celebrate their uniqueness and their differences—you are the best gifts God could have given me.

My special thanks to Victor Oliver and Kristen Lucas for all their hard work, feedback, input, and support through the entire process.

Finally, I offer my thanks to the people who have allowed me to take them on a journey to wholeness and well-being from these sacred texts. In spite of the many mistakes I have often made in the process of leading them into the future, the people I pastor at the Master's Touch have proven again and again that God has made them princes and princesses. They have offered me the opportunity to discover that these truths work again and again when there is a genuine atmosphere of faith, hope, and love.